Party Ideas

FOR CHILDREN

Dedicated to Nicholas and Amy –
their input and assistance was invaluable!

JENNY DODD

ACKNOWLEDGEMENTS

To Linda de Villiers for affording me the opportunity to produce this book and encouraging and motivating me from the very beginning. To Joy Clack for all the difficult and frustrating hours spent on this production – her expertise and professionalism was much appreciated and has taught me so much! Without her this book would have been impossible. To Beverley Dodd for planting the seed and then having the daunting task of nurturing it, through what were, at times, very trying situations – thank you Bev, your creative talent and experience have proved a real asset to me! To my husband, Cedric, for all the assistance he so readily provided throughout. To Natalie and Yvonne for delighting in my achievement, thank you so much for the support! Lastly to our two standard poodles – thank you for only eating one cake that had been set aside to cool!

JENNY DODD

Note: While every effort has been made to ensure that the information contained in this book is accurate, the author and publishers accept no responsibility for any loss, injury or inconvenience sustained by any person using this book or following the advice given in it.

First published in 2005 by Struik Publishers
(a division of New Holland Publishing (South Africa) (Pty) Ltd)
Cape Town • London • Sydney • Auckland
www.struik.co.za

Cornelis Struik House, 80 McKenzie Street,
Cape Town 8001, South Africa
Garfield House, 86–88 Edgware Road,
London W2 2EA, United Kingdom
14 Aquatic Drive, Frenchs Forest, NSW 2086, Australia
218 Lake Road, Northcote, Auckland, New Zealand

New Holland Publishing is a member
of Johnnic Communications Ltd

Hardcover edition ISBN 1 86872 966 4
Softcover edition ISBN 1 74110 458 0
2 3 4 5 6 7 8 9 10

PUBLISHING MANAGER: Linda de Villiers

EDITOR: Joy Clack

DESIGNER: Beverley Dodd

PHOTOGRAPHERS: Christoph and Diane Heierli

STYLIST: Abigail Donnelly

STYLIST'S ASSISTANT: Talia Prince

CAKE DECORATION: Abigail Donnelly, Talia Prince,
  Beverley Dodd, Joy Clack

ILLUSTRATOR: Janine Cloete

PROOFREADER: Tessa Kennedy

Reproduction by Hirt & Carter Cape (Pty) Ltd
Printed and bound by Craft (Pte) Ltd, Singapore

CONTENTS

INTRODUCTION

For my sixth birthday party I was able to invite a few friends home from school. Together with a neighbour, we were six in total. I can recall the excitement and just how very special I felt as the birthday girl.

There was much cheerful twittering as we all changed into our party clothes. One of the girls had a red polka-dot dress with a matching red hair ribbon and requested that my mother assist her with replacing the navy blue school ribbon that she wore. As the party progressed, my mother was obviously far too engrossed in the activities and all thoughts of the red ribbon were set aside.

I clearly recall how anxious I felt when my guest came up to me and announced that my mother had yet to fulfil her obligations concerning the red ribbon. This incident was of great concern to me even at that young age, as I couldn't bear the thought that one of my guests might have experienced disappointment. Fortunately, black-and-white photographs saved the day, for when we eventually received the pictures that had been taken, the navy ribbon was reflected in the same shade as the dress!

So, what's the moral of the story? Children *do* care and *do* want the party to be a success. They do care about the wellbeing of their guests and do want them to feel special.

Birthdays are always anticipated with a great deal of excitement and the planning and preparations for this special day contribute greatly to the enjoyment of the happy occasion. A well-planned party is also long remembered and appreciated. It is with all this in mind that I have endeavoured to provide a guide for children's parties that will contribute much to the excitement as the birthday child watches cake flour, icing sugar and sweets being transformed into fantasy. Involve the child in all the preparations and allow his or her input, respecting your child's opinions and suggestions.

Finally, remember to record the happy event by taking an abundance of photographs and include a video as well, if possible. These will provide treasured memories that will last forever (and dispel any recollections of toil and trouble!).

PARTY PREPARATIONS

Plan ahead and make the cake well in advance and not on the day of the party! Once the cake has been iced it may be covered with a large plastic bag and frozen until the day before the party, when the finishing touches may be added.

Cupcakes, for example, may also be made in advance and frozen, again adding the final decorations the day before the party. The same procedure may be applied to the biscuits.

PARTY THEMES

The themes depicted in this book can be achieved relatively quickly and at a low cost, but you may wish to adapt them to suit personal time and budget constraints. I haven't included specific themes for 1–2 year olds as their parties normally take the form of get-togethers for family and friends. However, the majority of the cakes will make an eye-catching centrepiece on their birthday table as well. You may wish to include some of the other recipes for older children who may be present.

PARTY DÉCOR

Setting the scene for the party need not be a formidable chore. The basic décor will always include streamers and balloons. Streamers (50 mm wide) cut from sheets of crepe paper are easy to make and, when twisted before hanging, create a wonderful canopy that can reflect the dominant colours of the theme.

Balloons always add extra appeal to any party. It has become standard practice to tie a bunch to the garden gate, allowing easy identification of the party venue. This gesture helps to make the birthday child feel extra special as the rest of the neighbourhood realises that a party is occurring at their home.

Tie balloons in bunches (the theme will determine the colours) in the corners of the party room, and wherever else the children are likely to gather. Add curling ribbons to enhance the festive appearance. Take care of broken bits of balloon and dispose of them immediately as they may be dangerous if swallowed. I have added extra tips for décor under each theme.

INVITATIONS

Always send out the invitations about two weeks before the day of the party, and remember to include an RSVP date, which will assist with the catering and the preparation of the games. Do phone up the moms who haven't replied to ascertain whether their child will be accepting the invitation.

Give the birthday child the guest list so that he or she may participate and tick off the names as the replies are received.

Apart from the starting time, stipulate the time that the party will end so that parents collect the children punctually. Ensure that the duration of the party is not too long – two hours is sufficient for most parties – to prevent children tiring and becoming bored.

Try to make the invitations original and creative, but if time is limited, ready-made invitations offer an easy alternative. I have included invitations in each theme with easy step-by-step instructions for how to put them together. I have endeavoured to keep them simple, yet appealing, so that the birthday child may assist in making them. I have also included ideas for the wording of the invitation details.

TREAT BAGS

These are great as they enable children to take home any party favours that they have accumulated. Instead of setting out all the food on the table, you may prefer to insert the sweets and small packets of crisps into the treat bags, to be enjoyed at the children's leisure. They are also ideal for a slice of birthday cake (wrapped in a serviette, of course).

The treat bags may always be recycled by the guest and used as preferred. More durable containers, such as those used in the Pink party (page 64), may be used as a container for pencils. The bags that have to be sewn take just a few minutes to complete and the materials are available at a reasonable price.

DRESSING UP

Most children enjoy fancy dress parties, but if you decide to add this stipulation to the invitation, remember to keep the expectations simple to ensure that all the children will be able to participate. It is a good idea to keep one or two clothing items or accessories on hand to assist children who fail to arrive in fancy dress.

PARTY FOOD

The techniques I have used for the cakes and other goodies are very simple and require only basic decorating tools. A toothpick and a pair of tweezers are invaluable aids. For icing, the star nozzle is a favourite of mine as I believe that it provides a neater and more attractive overall appearance. It is, however, more time-consuming. Sugar paste is readily available at baking supply stores, is very user-friendly and can easily be coloured using powdered food colourings.

I have used a limited range of ingredients (cupcakes, cones and biscuits for example) and adapted them with ease according to the theme. The cones provide an appealing display because of their height.

I have included more recipes than may be necessary for each theme, to allow a greater variety. Quantities for recipes in the party food section are not provided as these will vary according to the number of guests.

To enhance the visual impact of the party food, I use simple toys and take advantage of the huge selection of sweets that are available from speciality stores and supermarkets. I buy inexpensive toys throughout the year, as I find it impossible to pass by a toy shop or toy aisle, and I am able to purchase very useful items at reasonable prices. Toys transform any cake into an eye-catching centrepiece, and may also be used for prizes and party favours. I have sometimes planned an entire theme around a special toy that I have purchased.

GAMES AND ACTIVITIES

I have suggested that the winner receives a prize and the rest receive a small token. These may be in the form of stickers or an eraser, or anything inexpensive, to ensure that none of the children feel excluded.

The games have been provided as inspiration and to assist busy parents. You may prefer to hire entertainment.

THANK-YOU NOTES

These are a courteous gesture that children should adopt from an early age. Choosing a gift requires a lot of time and thought and the guest will be delighted to receive a note of thanks. Keep the note short and, if possible, have the birthday child write it personally. Keep a list of the gifts and who gave them – do this while the birthday child opens the gifts, otherwise it may be difficult to recall who gave what.

When planning a pool party, always ensure that strict adult supervision is maintained for the entire duration of the party, and stress this fact with the parents. Keep the guest numbers low.

Splash

SETTING THE SCENE

★ It is essential to have more than one helper. Wear a whistle as children have difficulty hearing instructions when they are in the water.

★ Find out from parents beforehand which children are unable to swim (children may be too shy to admit this in front of their peers) and provide safe and dependable swimming aids.

★ Lay a blue or light green cloth over the party table and cover with a piece of blue tulle, scrunched up in parts to resemble water. Scatter sea world confetti and/or shredded glitter foil on the table.

★ Decorate the party area with blue and green balloons and drape blue and green streamers above the party table. Serve the party food from beach buckets and sand modelling moulds.

★ Wind blue streamers through shrubs and place beach umbrellas in the garden to provide shady areas for the children and to enhance the summery theme.

★ Have separate changing rooms signposted 'Hunky lifeguards' for the boys, and 'Bathing belles' for the girls.

★ Have a back-up plan in case of bad weather on the day of the party – show a video or play games from some of the other themes in this book.

Recommended age group: 6–12

Splash

INVITATIONS

YOU WILL NEED:
Sunvisor template (page 157)
Scissors
Stiff card, colour of choice
Paper punch
Elastic cord
Glitter glue
Smiley sun template (page 157)
Bright yellow construction paper
Black and red felt-tip markers
Pair of googly eyes for each visor
Glitter
Craft glue

1. Enlarge the sunvisor template to the preferred size, cut it out and trace onto the stiff card. Cut out.
2. Punch a hole near each rounded end and thread the elastic through these, tying a knot to secure (adjust the elastic to fit a child's head).
3. Use glitter glue to write the guest's name. Write the invitation details (*see* Suggested wording) on the underside of the visor.
4. Enlarge the smiley sun template to the preferred size, cut it out and trace onto the yellow construction paper. Add the details with a felt-tip marker.
5. Attach the googly eyes and colour the mouth red. Decorate the rays with glitter. Glue the sun to the sun visor. (If you want smiley suns for the treat bags, make extra now.)

SUGGESTED WORDING

Help (birthday child's name) make a big splash!
Date:
Pool location: (address)
Pool opens: (time party starts)
Pool closes: (time party ends)
RSVP: lifeguard at (phone number) by (date)
Please bring bathing costume, towel and sun block.

TREAT BAGS

YOU WILL NEED:
Kiddies' plastic beach buckets (available at discount stores)
Curling ribbon
Coloured card
Smiley suns (optional)

1. Tie curling ribbon to the beach bucket handles.
2. Attach the guest's name to a matching coloured card.
3. Attach a smiley sun, if using.

OR
Empty, cleaned 1-litre yoghurt containers
Non-toxic craft spray paint
Coloured cord
Curling ribbon
Coloured card

1. Spray the yoghurt containers with craft spray.
2. Make two holes opposite each other just beneath the rim of the container and insert a piece of cord for the handle.
3. Decorate with ribbons and attach name cards.

GAMES AND ACTIVITIES

Photo shoots

This activity should take place as the children arrive so that, if possible, a helper can take the photos to a nearby 1-hour photo lab for processing. The pictures could then be ready for the children to take home when they leave the party. Alternatively, the pictures may be attached to the thank-you note. Remember to have two sets processed so that the birthday child has a set to keep!

YOU WILL NEED:
Two poster boards
Camera

Choose two poster boards that would be an appropriate size for the children.

Draw a strongman, flexing his muscles, for the boys, and a bikini girl for the girls. Colour and decorate, and cut out the faces. The children may stand behind them to have their photos taken.

Pin the tail on the fish

YOU WILL NEED:
Poster board
Construction paper
Double-sided tape
Blindfold

Draw a colourful fish, without a tail, on the poster board. Use a separate piece of stiff paper to make the tail and make sufficient so that each child has his or her own. Attach a small piece of double-sided tape to the back of each tail and write the child's name on the front.

Blindfold each child in turn, spin them about three times, then let them take their turn to attach the tail to the fish. The nearest correct tail wins a prize – the rest of the children may choose a smaller party treat from a beach bucket.

Catch the waterball

YOU WILL NEED:
Balloons filled with water

Group the children into pairs, with each pair receiving a water balloon. They must face each other at a distance of one metre apart. On starter's orders, one child must throw the balloon to the other. Those who catch the balloon without it bursting, move a step further away from their partner. Unsuccessful pairs are eliminated. The game continues until a winning pair is left.

Deep-sea fishing

YOU WILL NEED (PER TEAM):
Kiddies' inflatable life ring
Plastic bowl large enough to fit in the life ring
Small plastic fish

Divide the children into two teams. Provide each team with a bowl that is supported adrift in the water in the centre of an inflatable life ring. Throw plastic fish into the pool and, on starter's orders, the children must retrieve the fish and place them into their team's bowl.

After a specified time, the team that has the most fish in their bowl wins a prize. The rest receive tokens.

Musical towels

YOU WILL NEED:
Music
Towels (one less than the number of children)

Spread out the towels. The children must dance while moving around the towels. When the music stops, they must rush to a towel – the child without one is out. The game continues with a towel being removed at the start of each round, until there is a winner.

PARTY FOOD

Sunshine cones

Wafer ice-cream cones
Marie biscuits or Rich Tea™ biscuits
Icing (page 152) – orange, blue, red
Small sweets of choice
Round apricot sweets
Gold balls

1. Remove the greater part of the tapered section of an ice-cream cone, slicing it at a slight angle.
2. Place a blob of icing on one side of a Marie or tea biscuit and position it on the cut edge of the cone. Fill the cone with small sweets, then place the base of the cone on a second Marie or tea biscuit and secure that with icing too.
3. Cut an apricot sweet in half and place, cut side down, on the top biscuit with a blob of icing.
4. Using the star nozzle and orange icing, create the sun rays.
5. Decorate the face of the sun as illustrated.
6. Pipe orange stars around the base of the cone and enhance with gold balls.

Aquarium cakes

Party Cupcakes (page 153)
Icing (page 152) – blue, colour of choice
Silver balls
Jelly Beans™

1. Bake the cupcakes according to the recipe and allow to cool completely before covering with blue icing.
2. Trace the outline of a fish on each cake with a toothpick, and fill in using the star decorating nozzle. Position a silver ball for the eye.
3. Use halved Jelly Beans™ for the pebbles on the 'sea bed'.

Bathing hunks or belles

Easy Biscuits (page 152)
Gingerbread man cookie cutter
Icing (page 152) – colours of choice
Gold balls

1. Prepare the biscuit dough according to the recipe.
2. Cut out the biscuits with the cookie cutter and bake as directed. Allow to cool completely.
3. Decorate as illustrated.

Catch of the day

Needle and thread
Fish-shaped jelly sweets
Chocolate-dipped pretzel sticks
Blue ice cream
Sugar cones

1. Use a sterile needle to pass a piece of thread through one end of a fish sweet. Knot to secure, then tie the thread to the pretzel stick.
2. Place two scoops of ice cream into a sugar cone and insert the 'fishing rod' just before serving.

Tropical fruit medley

Bath sponges
Watermelon balls
Melon balls
Strawberries
Kiwi fruit, sliced
Wooden skewers

1. Purchase bath sponges in sea theme shapes and insert toothpicks skewered with the prepared fruits.
2. You may wish to purchase sufficient sponges so that each child receives their own to take home.

ROCK POOL CAKE

1 x Basic Cake (page 152) – 330 x 260 mm cake
1 x packet blue jelly (powder or cubes)
Clear, shallow plastic bowl about 150 mm in diameter
Icing (page 152) – chocolate, green, pale brown
2 x Marie biscuits or Rich Tea™ biscuits, crushed
2 Tbsp (30 ml) desiccated coconut, coloured green
Chocolate oat drops (page 153) – use half quantity
Small round sweets for beach balls
Small dolls of choice
Paper parasols
Plastic sea creatures
Large dome-shaped sugared jelly sweets
Candy sticks

1. Bake the cake as per the recipe and allow to cool.
2. Mix the blue jelly according to the package instructions and allow to set in the fridge.
3. Position the plastic bowl near the one short edge of the cake and carefully cut out a hole to accommodate the bowl.
4. Use the cut-out section to extend the overall length of the cake by positioning the pieces along the surrounding edge of the rock pool – don't fuss about it being uneven as this is the desired effect with a rock pool.
5. Mark out a section of lawn as well as a section of sand on the other side of the cake.
6. Cover the section surrounding the pool with chocolate icing, the lawn with green icing and the sand with a pale brown icing.
7. Cover the sandy section with crushed Marie or tea biscuits and the lawn with green coconut.
8. Use chocolate oat drops to create rocks, and position these around the pool.
9. Decorate the cake using toys and position the round sweets for beach balls.
10. Attach the dome-shaped sweets to the candy sticks with a dab of icing to create shrubs, and position these on the lawn.
11. Just before the party, chop up the jelly and add it to the plastic bowl. Position more toys in the 'water'.

SETTING THE SCENE

- It is more practical to have this party outdoors or on a patio as it could be rather 'muddy'. The children will relish the idea of being able to take a present home for their parents, and their happy faces will compensate for any mess incurred!

- Use face paint to adorn the children's faces with an assortment of 'garden critters' as they arrive at the party, or use fake tattoos if preferred.

- Tie balloons together with curling ribbon and hang them from the trees and shrubs in the garden and/or the ceiling. Make suns, ladybugs, butterflies and bees using poster paper and suspend from the ceiling or position in the garden, allowing them to 'fly' over the party area.

- Cover the table with a green cloth and, if possible, sprinkle with petals and leaves. Place fresh flowers on the table and throughout the activity area. Alternatively, cut out paper flowers.

- Serve drinks from clean plastic watering cans (tie ribbon around the handles) and serve food from baskets, toy wheelbarrows, plastic garden pots, and so on.

- Apart from the party table, set up a low potting table. Cover with green crepe paper, make large sunflowers from yellow and brown construction paper (use the template provided), and glue them to the crepe paper. Finally cover the whole table with clear plastic sheeting.

- Provide the children with a plastic flowerpot marked with their names at their place settings.

- Wrap the pot in a Cellophane bundle and tie with a bright ribbon. Insert a 'wind flower' toy through the opening so that it is supported in an upright position.

- Place the seedlings to be planted down the centre of the table. These will be seasonal, but choose seedlings that have flowers. Impatiens, for example, always provide a lovely show.

- Position buckets of soil on the side, as well as drainage stones, fertilizer and watering cans.

Recommended age group: 4-8

Garden

INVITATIONS

YOU WILL NEED:
Sunflower template (page 156)
Scissors
Bright yellow crepe paper
Pen or pencil
Craft glue
Glitter glue
Stiff brown paper
Sunflower seeds
Green pipe cleaners
Wooden skewers
Masking tape
Notepaper
Green curling ribbon

1. Enlarge the template to the preferred size, cut out and trace two sunflowers onto the crepe paper. Cut out.
2. Place one on top of the other, rotating the upper section slightly to create a double row of petals. Spread glue in the centre and join the two sections, leaving the petals free to blow in the wind.
3. Decorate the petals using glitter glue.
4. Trace the centre circle of the sunflower onto the stiff brown paper, cover with glue and attach the sunflower seeds. Coat the seeds with glitter glue.
5. Set aside to dry, then attach the central section to the centre of the petals using the craft glue.
6. Wind a pipe cleaner around a wooden skewer and attach it to the back of the flower head using a piece of masking tape.
7. Write the invitation details on notepaper (*see* Suggested wording) and attach it to the skewer using a green, trailing curling ribbon.

SUGGESTED WORDING
Exercise green fingers at (child's name)'s gardening party!
Nursery: party venue
Blooms open: (start of party)
Blooms close: (end of party)
RSVP: head gardener at (phone number) by (date)
Dress: gardening clothes, sun hats and aprons

TREAT BAGS

YOU WILL NEED:
Same as for the invitations, omitting the stem
Bright green gift bags
Green and brown or gold streamers
Masking tape
Craft glue

1. Follow steps 1–5 of the invitation instructions.
2. Attach long green and brown or gold streamers to the back of the sunflower with a small piece of masking tape and attach the sunflower to the gift bag with glue so that the streamers trail from behind the flower to resemble roots.

GAMES AND ACTIVITIES

As the children will spend some time planting their seedlings, not many games are necessary.

Pluck a petal

YOU WILL NEED:
Daisy-type flower (use two if the group is large)
Music

Instruct the children to sit in a circle and pass a flower from one to the other while the music plays.

When the music stops, the child holding the flower must carefully remove one petal. The game continues until the winning child plucks the last petal.

Beetle drive

YOU WILL NEED:
Paper
Dice
Pencils

Divide the children into groups of four or five.

Provide each group with a dice and each child with a sheet of paper and a pencil.

The children throw the dice in succession and the game is rated as follows: 1 = body, 2 = head, 3 = an eye, 4 = antenna, 5 = tail, 6 = leg. A body (1) must be thrown to start, followed by a 2 for the head, and so on.

The first child in each group to complete a beetle wins a prize and the remaining children receive tokens.

PARTY FOOD

Fragrant flowers

Sliced, buttered bread
Sandwich fillings of choice
Shredded lettuce
Chopped fresh parsley
Radishes

1. Use a variety of fillings that children enjoy – ham and mustard, cheese, tuna, chicken or egg mayonnaise, fish paste, and so on.
2. After assembling the sandwiches, cut out shapes with a flower-shaped cookie cutter and decorate with a round of cheese in the centre.
3. Garnish the serving platter with shredded lettuce, finely chopped parsley and radishes.

Sneaky snails

Meringues (page 153)
Hundreds and thousands
Silver balls

1. Prepare the meringue mixture according to the recipe, then use a wide star-shaped nozzle to pipe a snail shape onto a baking tray lined with greaseproof paper.
2. Sprinkle the shell section with hundreds and thousands and position silver balls for eyes.
3. Bake as directed.

A buggy delivery

Half a cabbage
Small apple
Toothpicks
Edible (wafer) cookie cup
Cherry tomato
Cocktail onions
Red pepper strip
6 x 150 mm lengths of pipe cleaner
Sausage flowers (see directions below)

1. To make the bug, place the cabbage, cut side down, on a serving board.
2. Cut a slice off the bottom side of a small apple to level the base and attach the apple to the core side of the cabbage using a toothpick.
3. Place an upturned cookie cup on the apple to make a hat. Spear a cherry tomato on one end of a toothpick and stick it through the centre of the cookie cup to secure the hat to the apple. Attach cocktail onion eyes and a red pepper strip as a mouth to the apple using toothpicks.
4. Attach the pipe cleaner legs, sticking three on each side, into the cabbage, about 40 mm from the lower edge, bending each slightly in the centre so that the outer edges touch the serving board and appear to support the critter.
5. Insert the sausage flowers into the cabbage to create a floral display.

Sausage flowers

1. Cut the rounded ends off the sausage (eg: frankfurter or vienna), then cut the sausage into 25 mm lengths.
2. Cut diagonally three times into one end of each sausage, thus creating six separate 'petals'.
3. Plunge into a saucepan of boiling water for a few minutes to allow the 'petals' to open. Drain well.
4. Fix onto a toothpick and attach a coloured cocktail onion to form the centre of the flower.
5. Use different colours to maximize the effect.

Croaking critter

Easy Biscuits (page 152)
Lily pad template (page 156)
Icing (page 152) – dark green
Plastic toy frogs
Marshmallow flowers (page 153)
Jelly Tots™

1. Prepare the biscuit dough as per the recipe.
2. Trace the template onto stiff paper, cut it out and use this template to cut out the biscuits – 1 x recipe yields about 16.
3. Bake as directed and leave to cool completely.
4. Decorate with dark green icing and trace leaf veins using a toothpick.
5. Position the toy frog and marshmallow flower.
6. Place the Jelly Tot™, flat side down, in the centre of the flower.

Pretty maids in a row

Party Cupcakes (page 153)
Marshmallow Flowers (page 153)
Lollipops
Icing (page 152) – dark green
Desiccated coconut, coloured green
Vermicelli balls
Sugared worm-shaped sweets
Coloured balls

1. Bake the cupcakes according to the recipe and leave to cool completely.
2. Make marshmallow petals as directed and attach to the lollipop with icing.
3. 'Cement' with extra icing at the back of the lollipop and leave to set in the fridge.
4. Ice the cupcakes roughly with dark green icing, and sprinkle with coloured coconut and vermicelli balls. Position a sugared worm and a little flower made from coloured balls.
5. Lastly add the lollipop flower.

SAMMY THE SCARECROW CAKE

2 x Basic Cake (page 152) – place one mixture in a 330 x 260 mm cake tin, and divide
  the second mixture between one x 200 mm round tin and one x 220 mm square tin

Icing (page 152) – flesh-coloured, brown, red, blue, white

16 x Liquorice Allsorts Mini™

2 x round yellow sweets

Plain and chocolate-dipped pretzel sticks

1 x liquorice strip

1 x large dome-shaped sugared jelly sweet

2 x large googly eyes

Lollipop or artificial sunflower

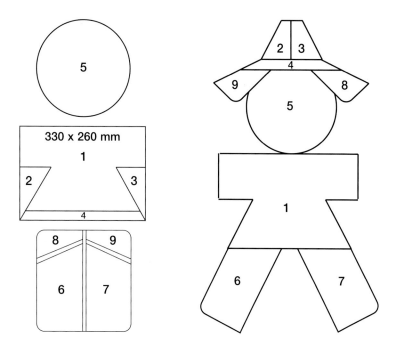

1. Bake the cakes as directed and allow to cool completely.

2. Cut out and assemble according to the templates. (1 = bodice; 2 & 3 = peaked crown of hat,
   cut top ends straight across; 4 = brim of hat, ends trimmed to fit; 5 = face; 6 & 7 = legs;
   8 & 9 = sides of hat.)

3. Ice the cake as follows: flesh-coloured icing for the face, brown icing for the hat with an iced
   red band, blue icing for the dungarees, red and white icing for the checked shirt.

4. Use the Liquorice Allsorts Mini™ to make the patch on the dungarees and the round yellow sweets
   for the buttons.

5. Insert the pretzel sticks for the hands and feet. Use the chocolate-dipped pretzels for the hair.

6. Decorate the face as follows: strip of liquorice for the mouth; sugared jelly sweet for the nose; googly eyes.

7. Stick the lollipop or sunflower into the hat.

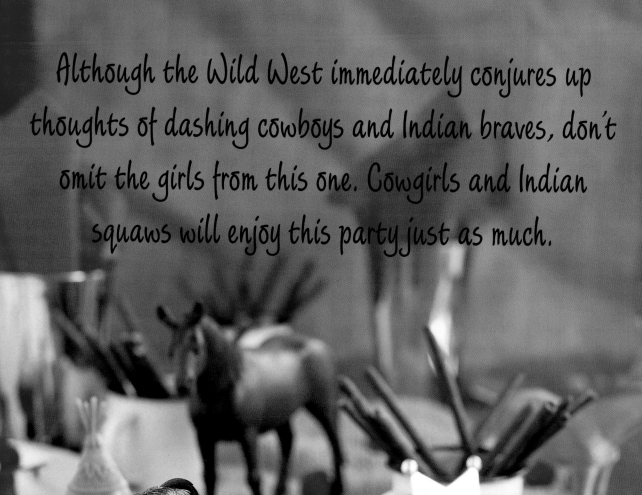

Although the Wild West immediately conjures up thoughts of dashing cowboys and Indian braves, don't omit the girls from this one. Cowgirls and Indian squaws will enjoy this party just as much.

The Wild

SETTING THE SCENE

* Cut out horseshoe shapes from construction paper, spray them silver and lay a trail from the garden gate to the party room.

* Use face paint to give the Indians 'face stripes' and the cowboys 'moustaches' as they arrive.

* Hang plenty of red balloons from the ceiling and drape red streamers from the centre to the corners of the room.

* Hang hessian cloth against the walls and create a few 'Wanted' and 'Reward' posters to attach to the cloth.

* Drape the party table with a hessian cloth and serve food from foil or tin plates.

* You may also use upturned toy cowboy hats for serving chips and sweets.

* Serve drinks from enamel mugs or use plastic mugs with handles.

Recommended age group: 4-10

Wild West

INVITATIONS

YOU WILL NEED (PER INVITATION):
20–25 cm length of leather thong, or cord of choice
2 or more beads, as preferred, to fit the cord
1 x feather
1 x metal attachment for securing feather to the
thong (available from bead shops)
Stiff card
Paper punch
Hair clip
(optional)

1. Thread the beads onto one end of the cord, then thread the end of the cord and feather through the metal attachment and clamp to secure it to the end of cord.
2. Write the invitation details (*see* Suggested wording) on the card, punch a hole and attach to the other end of the cord and knot it.
3. Attach a hair clip to the free end of the cord if it is to be worn to the party.

SUGGESTED WORDING
Saddle up for (birthday child's name)'s birthday party!
Corral: (party address)
Round up: (date and times)
RSVP: sheriff at (phone number) by (date)
Dress: Western – remember to wear the headband to the party!

TREAT BAGS

YOU WILL NEED (PER BAG):
Hessian material, prewashed, measuring
200 mm x 440 mm
Needle and thread
Paper
Fabric paint
Cord
Sheriff's badge
(optional)

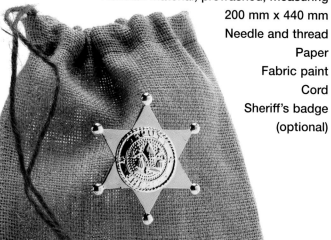

1. Fold the material in half and sew the two sides together, leaving the top open.
2. Fold under about 20 mm and hem to make a casing, leaving a small section open to thread the cord through.
3. Insert a piece of paper into the bag (to prevent the paint from seeping through) and use the fabric paint to write the guest's name. Allow to dry.
4. Thread the cord through the casing and tie the ends of the cord together.
5. Attach a sheriff's badge to the bag if desired.

GAMES AND ACTIVITIES

Panning for gold

YOU WILL NEED:
Kiddies' wading pool
Beach sand
Foil plates with a few holes punched in them
Gold stones such as those used in aquariums or
    spray paint small stones

Set up the wading pool, pour in a fair amount of sand and add water to fill. Allow the children a time limit to pan for gold (an egg-timer may help).
   As soon as a child finds a gold 'nugget', they must stop panning and trade their gold for a prize chosen from a basket.

Floating feather

YOU WILL NEED:
Feathers

Divide the children into small groups and provide each group with a feather. On starter's orders, the children have to keep their feathers in the air by blowing at them.
   The winning group (the one who keeps the feather aloft for the longest time) wins a prize. After the game, hand each child a feather to take home.

Cowboy and Indian war dance

YOU WILL NEED:
Balloons
Country and Western music

Mark out the dance area. Tie a balloon to each child's ankle. The children must dance to Country and Western music, attempting to pop each other's balloons while at the same time protecting their own.
   As each balloon is popped, the child is eliminated. The winner receives a prize, the rest receive a token.

Sharpshooters

YOU WILL NEED:
Water pistols
Target of choice

Instruct the children to stand behind a predetermined mark and take turns to shoot at the target.
   With each round, the child furthest from the target is eliminated and the mark is moved about 500 mm further away from the target.
   The winner receives a prize, the rest receive a token.

The sheriff says . . .

The sheriff (an adult volunteer) stands in front of the group of children and calls out instructions. The group must follow only those instructions that are preceded by 'The Sheriff says...'.
   Those children who mimic the actions without the necessary phrase are eliminated. The winner receives a prize, the rest receive a token.

PARTY FOOD

Pony express

Sliced, buttered bread
Sandwich fillings of choice
Piece of cardboard, covered with aluminium foil, for
   the serving platter
4 x thick slices of tomato
4 x toothpicks
4 x green cocktail onions
2 x wooden skewers
Prestik® or Blu-tac™
1 x toy horse

1. Remove the crusts from the bread and prepare an
   assortment of evenly sized, rectangular sandwiches.
2. Arrange them in a rectangular pattern on the
   platter, about 25 cm in length and about three
   rows high (depending, of course, on the number
   of guests).
3. Skewer a thick slice of tomato on each of four
   toothpicks to form wheels, and place in position.
4. Add a green cocktail onion to cover the end of
   the toothpick.
5. Use Prestik® or Blu-tac™ to attach the wooden
   skewers to the sides of the horse. Place the horse
   in front of the cart to enable it to 'pull' the wagon.

Prairie punch

MAKES 3.5 LITRES
1 litre orange juice
1 litre pineapple juice
1.5 litres lemonade

1. Mix together the two fruit juices in a large
   plastic bucket.
2. Add the lemonade and some ice cubes just
   before serving with a ladle.

Longhorn lassoes

The birthday child can help prepare these!

Prepared popcorn
Elastic thread – 750 mm per lasso
Thick sterile sewing needle

1. Thread the popcorn onto the elastic thread using
   the needle.
2. After 500 mm has been threaded, form a loop
   and knot the thread to secure.
3. Continue to thread the remaining section of the
   lasso and knot the end.

Bucking bronco boots

Easy Biscuits (page 152)
Boot template (page 156)
Melted baking chocolate
Star-shaped sweets
Banana-shaped sweets

1. Prepare the biscuit dough as per the recipe.
2. Trace the template onto stiff paper, cut it out
   and use this template to cut out the biscuits.
3. Bake as directed and allow to cool completely.
4. Coat with the melted chocolate and leave to set.
5. Place the sweets in position to make the spurs,
   securing them with a little melted chocolate.

Other food ideas

Cowpoke corn: layer corn chips on an ovenproof
platter, sprinkle with grated cheese and place under
the grill until the cheese has melted.
Apache arrows: place meatballs and cherry tomatoes
onto skewers and attach a wedge of cheese for the
arrowhead. Add a paper frill at the other end.

WILD WEST CAKE

2 x Basic Cake (page 152) – each 330 mm x 260 mm cakes
Icing (page 152) – blue, green, light brown, white
2 x Marie biscuits or Rich Tea™ biscuits, crushed and lightly coloured with a pinch of cocoa powder
4 x edible (wafer) cookie cups
Sprinkling of desiccated coconut
Chocolate Crispies (page 153)
2 x small ready-made swiss rolls
Wooden skewers
Liquorice Allsorts Mini™
Star-shaped sweets
Large dome-shaped sugared jelly sweets
1 x wafer biscuit
Florist's wire with three rings attached
Polyester fibre filling
Plastic toys of choice

1. Bake the cakes as per the recipe and allow to cool completely.
2. Place the cakes side by side to form a large rectangle.
3. With a toothpick, mark out a river, slightly off centre, as illustrated. Ice with blue icing.
4. Use green icing to coat the smaller cowboy section, and light brown icing for the Indian camp. Sprinkle the crushed Marie or tea biscuits over the surface of the Indian camp to create an arid environment.
5. Place three wafer cookie cups upside down in the back right-hand corner of the Indian camp (to create a hill), trimming slightly to fit alongside each other, and coat with light brown icing.
6. Place the remaining cookie cup upside down at the top end of the river, and ice blue, to create a waterfall.
7. Sprinkle white coconut at the base of the waterfall and also along the river.
8. Line the riverbanks with chocolate crispies and sprinkle a few pieces at the top of the waterfall.
9. Assemble the totem pole by skewering the two swiss rolls (trim the skewer to fit) and insert into the cake.
10. Ice as illustrated, and use the Liquorice Allsorts Mini™, and the star- and dome-shaped sweets for decoration.
11. Cut a wafer biscuit in half horizontally and then shape the wings as illustrated.
12. Gently insert one end of a toothpick into each of the wings and insert the other end into the swiss roll.
13. Insert florist's wire and attach fibre filling to the rings to create the smoke signals.
14. Arrange the other toys as illustrated.

This party is a 'girls only' affair! The theme lends itself to fancy dress, which is relatively easy as most little girls have fairy outfits. And they may use their invitation wands to complete the outfit!

SETTING THE SCENE

* Decorate the party room with metallic silver balloons and another dominant colour of choice – for this example I have used lilac.

* Drape twisted lilac streamers from the centre of the ceiling to the corners.

* Use fishing line to suspend silver stars from the ceiling and paste large silver stars on the walls.

* Serve food from stars made from stiff board and sprayed lilac with non-toxic craft spray.

* Cover the party table with aluminium foil, shiny side uppermost. Scrunch a piece of lilac organza material or lilac tulle down the centre and sprinkle with lilac or fairy-shaped confetti.

* Have an extra fairy skirt or pair of wings available in case a child arrives without fancy dress.

* Tie a ribbon with a bell around the ankle of each child as they arrive and, using face paint, apply a little star or flower to cheeks. Adorn faces and limbs with body glitter.

* Shower the children with a sprinkling of confetti as they approach the party room.

Recommended age group: 3–6

Fairies

INVITATIONS

YOU WILL NEED (PER INVITATION):
Star template (page 156)
Stiff lilac card measuring 150 x 150 mm
Scissors
Sequins
Glitter
Craft glue
Prestik® or Blu-tac™
Thin dowel stick, about 250 mm long
Lilac craft paint or pipe cleaners
Notepaper
Curling ribbon

1. Enlarge the template to the preferred size and trace it onto the stiff card. Cut out and decorate with sequins and glitter.
2. Use Prestik® or Blu-tac™ to attach the star to the dowel stick that has been painted the same colour as the wand, or wind a pipe cleaner around the stick if preferred.
3. Write the party details (*see* Suggested wording) on the notepaper and attach it to the wand with matching curling ribbon.

SUGGESTED WORDING

Follow the fairy dust to (birthday child's name) party.
Fairyland: (address)
Time to make a wish come true: (date and times)
RSVP: fairy godmother at (phone number) by (date)
Dress: fairy fancy dress

TREAT BAGS

YOU WILL NEED (PER BAG):
Tulle or fabric of choice measuring 400 x 200 mm
Needle and thread
Length of cord or ribbon (same colour as the fabric)
Self-adhesive silver stars

1. Fold the material in half and sew together along the two side edges, leaving the top end open for the cord.
2. Turn down about 15 mm and hem to form a casing, leaving about 20 mm free to insert the cord or ribbon.
3. Thread the cord or ribbon through the casing, and knot the two ends together to secure.
4. Attach the stars to the front of the bag.

GAMES AND ACTIVITIES

Crowning glory

This activity should take place as soon as the children arrive so that, if possible, a helper can take the film to a nearby 1-hour photo lab for processing. The pictures could then be ready for the children to take home when they leave. Alternatively, the pictures may be attached to the thank-you note. Remember to have two sets processed so that the birthday child has a set to keep!

YOU WILL NEED:
Chair draped with lilac cloth, tinsel,
** ribbons and balloons**
Bottles of bubble fun
Plastic crown

The children form an aisle and blow bubbles as the birthday child approaches the throne to be crowned fairy queen. Allow the birthday child to sit on the throne while the crown is placed on her head. Take photographs of all the children in turn on the throne wearing the crown.

Fairy masks

YOU WILL NEED:
Plain masks available from party supply stores,
** or make your own using construction paper**
** and elastic thread**
Sequins
Glitter
Feathers
Beads
Pipe cleaners
Craft glue

Allow the little fairies to decorate their own masks. Set aside a low table where they may work. Drape with lilac crepe paper and cover with a clear plastic sheet. Arrange the accessory items in dainty matching bowls placed down the centre of the craft table, within easy reach of each fairy.

Magical fairy dells

The children will enjoy jingling their fairy bells as they dance and skip around the dells.

YOU WILL NEED:
Cardboard circles – ensure that there are sufficient,
** less one, for each child**
Lilac craft paint
Glitter
Music

Spray the cardboard circles lilac and sprinkle with glitter while still wet. Spread the circles (dells) on the ground and, as in musical chairs, have the children skip around them. When the music stops they must rush to a dell. The child without a dell is eliminated.

Remove a dell with each round as the game continues, with a child being eliminated in each round until there is a winner.

Fairy coronet race

YOU WILL NEED:
Tinsel coronets – one for each child

Divide the children into two teams and have two piles of coronets made from tinsel, big enough to fit snugly on each child's head.

Place the two piles at a predetermined distance from the children, who must line up one behind the other in their respective teams.

On starter's orders, the first child in each team runs to the pile, puts a coronet on her head, runs back without holding onto the coronet, touches the hand of the next fairy who repeats the procedure. If the coronet falls off, they must stop to put it back on their head.

The first team to have all their coronets in place wins a prize, the rest of the children receive a small token.

PARTY FOOD

Toadstools

Easy Biscuits (page 152)
Toadstool template (page 156)
Icing (page 152) – chocolate, lilac
Plastic ladybugs
Sweets of choice

1. Prepare the biscuit dough as per the recipe.
2. Enlarge the toadstool template to the preferred size, trace it onto cardboard and cut it out. Use the template to cut out biscuits and bake as directed.
3. Allow to cool completely before coating the stem with chocolate icing and the top with lilac icing.
4. Place the ladybug and sweets on the biscuit.

Fairy cakes

Party Cupcakes (page 153)
Icing (page 152) – lilac, white
Silver balls
Heart-shaped sugared jelly sweets

1. Bake the cupcakes in silver cookie cups (muffin cases) according to instructions and allow to cool.
2. Using the star nozzle, pipe on alternating lilac and white rounds. Decorate with silver balls and insert a toothpick topped with a heart-shaped sweet.

Other food ideas

Strawberry kebabs: skewered strawberries and marshmallows drizzled with melted chocolate.
Magic potions: grape and other purplish-coloured cold drinks; decorate straws with foil frills (page 154).
Blueberry ice cream: in sugar cones with edible glitter.
Pixie pleasures: marshmallow cones (page 153) decorated with edible glitter and silver dust.

Fairy queen

Wafer ice-cream cones
Small sweets of choice
Marie biscuits or Rich Tea™ biscuits
Icing (page 152) – yellow, lilac
Circle of tulle about 110 mm in diameter
Toothpicks and silver stars for wands (attach the stars with a small dot of Prestik® or Blu-tac™)
White gum balls or white marshmallows
Silver balls
Red food colouring
Thin silver string, cut into 5 cm lengths
Purple or silver star-shaped sweets

1. Fill the cone with small sweets. Coat a Marie or tea biscuit with icing and cover the cone, then upend so that the biscuit forms the base.
2. Fold the tulle circle in half and attach it to the cone using the wand to secure; insert the toothpick on one side of the cone and allow it to protrude slightly through the opposite side of the wing.
3. Remove the tip from the cone and set aside – this will be the hat.
4. Coat the open end of the cone with icing and attach a gum ball or marshmallow for the head.
5. Use yellow icing to add hair and use a small blob of icing to secure two silver balls for the eyes. Draw a thin red strip for the mouth using food colouring.
6. Make a small hole at the top end of the cone tip and insert the silver string. Push icing into the tip to secure the string.
7. Position the hat on the fairy's head.
8. Fix the purple stars in place using a little icing.
9. Finally ice the skirt and buttons as illustrated.

FAIRY CASTLE CAKE

2 x Basic Cake (page 152) – one x 250 mm round cake; two x 200 mm round cakes
Sugar paste – white
Icing sugar for dusting
Icing (page 152) – lilac
Half ready-made swiss roll
Mini chocolate slabs (or cut a large thin chocolate slab into equal-sized rectangles)
About 400 mm of silver cord
1 x wafer ice-cream cone
Large silver balls
Small silver balls
Small fairy dolls

1. Bake the cakes according to the recipe and allow to cool completely.
2. Roll out the sugar paste on a wooden board that has been lightly dusted with icing sugar and, using small flower cutters of different sizes (available from baking supply stores), press out as many flowers as necessary to decorate the cake.
3. Cut out a door as illustrated, as well as three windows (use a small icing tube to make the holes for the window panes).
4. Coat the larger cake with icing. Sandwich the two smaller cakes with a layer of icing, then position on top of the larger cake. Cover with icing.
5. Add the swiss roll to the top and cover with icing.
6. Place the mini chocolate slabs around the outer edge of the bottom layer.
7. Position the door and two windows on the middle tier, and place the window in position on the top tier.
8. Position the sugar paste flowers as illustrated.
9. Cut the cord into four pieces, each about 100 mm in length.
10. Pierce a hole in the top of the ice-cream cone and insert the thread. Secure with a blob of icing.
11. Coat the entire cone with icing and place on top of the cake.
12. Use the star nozzle to decorate the cake as illustrated, and add the silver balls and fairy dolls.

Ideally, this party is more fun if held outdoors. Children will be enthralled by their encounters with the creepy crawlies and, as the plastic toys are well priced in toy stores, it is possible to include quite a few party favours to add to their excitement.

creepy

SETTING THE SCENE

* Use construction paper to make an enormous butterfly or bug to attach to the front gate, together with balloons, to greet the children.

* This is a perfect party theme for face painting – if possible have a helper do this as the children arrive, or use face tattoos.

* Plastic bugs are readily available at discount toy stores and party stores – buy plenty and scatter throughout the house, including bathrooms.

* Display green balloons and drape green and brown streamers above the party table.

* Cover the party table with a green or yellow cloth or crepe paper, scatter with shredded green crepe paper or Cellophane wrap and place plastic bugs and other creepy crawlies in the 'grass'. Arrange washed garden stones on the table to provide hiding places for plastic spiders and snakes.

* Suspend plastic or cardboard bees and butterflies from the ceiling with fishing line.

* Tiny pot plants with hovering butterflies and ladybugs (attached to florist's wire or wooden skewers) will add to the theme.

* Suspend trails of ivy or other garden creepers in the doorway and position bugs and other spiders to 'greet' children as they pass through.

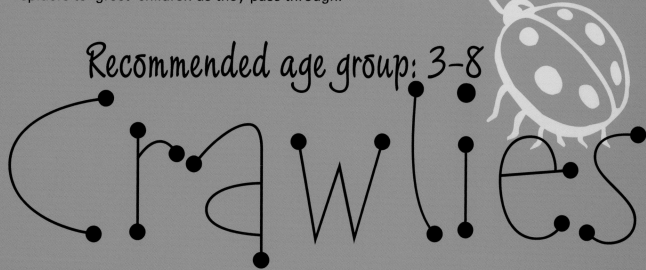

Recommended age group: 3-8

Crawlies

INVITATIONS

YOU WILL NEED:
Shredded green
crepe paper
Small plastic
containers with lids
Plastic bugs
and butterflies
Notepaper
Curling ribbon
Prestik® or
Blu-tac™

1. Place the shredded crepe paper inside the plastic container and add one or two toy insects.
2. Write the party details (*see* Suggested wording) on the notepaper, roll up, tie with a short length of curling ribbon and place inside the container.
3. Close the container and attach a plastic butterfly, together with a 'twist' of curling ribbon, to the lid, using a small ball of Prestik® or Blu-tac™ to secure.

SUGGESTED WORDING
Flutter by and join (birthday child's name)'s party!
Insect wonderland: (address)
Cocoons rupture: (date and times)
RSVP: buzz the queen bee at (phone number) by (date)
Dress: fancy dress is a good option for this party, as a simple pair of antennae, an all-black outfit and a pair of cardboard wings, for example, can transform the child into an awesome insect

TREAT BAGS

YOU WILL NEED (PER BAG):
2 x red or green disposable foam party plates
Scissors or craft knife
Brown pipe cleaner
Masking tape
Stiff green paper,
large enough to
make a leaf about
60 mm in length
Glitter glue
Prestik® or Blu-tac™
Sour or jelly worm-
shaped sweet
Stapler
Cord or pipe
cleaner for
handle
Plastic bug

1. Cut a slight indentation at the tops of the two plates so that the plates resemble an apple shape.
2. Make a hole near the top of one plate and insert a short length of pipe cleaner for the stalk. Secure it with masking tape on the inside of the plate.
3. Cut a leaf from the green paper, decorate with glitter glue, and attach to the stalk with Prestik® or Blu-tac™.
4. Make a hole in the front plate and position a protruding worm. Secure it with tape if necessary.
5. Use glitter glue to write the guest's name on the second plate.
6. Staple the plates together, leaving the top open.
7. Attach the cord handle.
8. Use Prestik® or Blu-tac™ to attach the plastic bug to the plate.

GAMES AND ACTIVITIES

Musical insects

YOU WILL NEED:
Cardboard
Scissors
Craft paints
Felt-tip markers
Music

Trace and cut out three different designs, about 30 cm across, on the cardboard: a flower, a leaf, and a spider web. Paint the shapes brightly and use felt-tip markers to add the details. Spread them on the ground, quite a distance from each other.

Play music while the children skip and dance about. When the music stops, the caller shouts either:
Bee – the children have to buzz to the flower shape;
Caterpillar – the children have to wriggle to the leaf;
Spider – the children have to jump to the web.
On reaching the relevant design, they have to form a circle around the cardboard shape. The last child to reach the assembled group is eliminated.

Bug hunt

YOU WILL NEED:
Plastic insects and snakes

Hide plastic toy creepy crawlies, butterflies, snakes and other little creatures in the garden. Ensure that there are sufficient for each child.

Once the children have located a creature, they are eliminated and can assist the other children in their search, thus ensuring that each child has a fair chance.

The children get to keep their creatures.

Bugstacle race

YOU WILL NEED:
Garden leaves
Water pistols
Bowl of sweets
Pot plant

Divide the children into two teams and mark a starting point. One child from each team must race through the obstacle course as follows:
– Crawl like caterpillars on their tummies through a pile of garden leaves.
– Jump like grasshoppers while two volunteers spray them using water pistols (insecticide).
– Collect pollen from a flower like a bee: position a flowering pot plant alongside a bowl of sweets – the child must select a sweet from the bowl and eat it before moving on to the finish line.
The next child starts as soon as the previous child finishes. Each child from the winning team receives a prize, the rest of the children receive tokens.

Insect statues

YOU WILL NEED:
Music

When the music starts, the children must dance in a circle pretending to be an insect (the game co-ordinator selects an insect with each round of play, and children mimic the noise and actions).

When the music stops, everybody must stop moving and stand as still and quiet as a statue. The first child who moves or makes a noise is eliminated. The game continues until there is a winner.

PARTY FOOD

Flutterbies

Party Cupcakes (page 153)
Icing (page 152) – colour of choice
Small worm-shaped jelly sweets
Heart-shaped sweets

1. Bake the cupcakes according to the recipe and allow to cool before coating with icing.
2. Attach a jelly worm and insert the heart-shaped sweets at a 45° angle to resemble wings.

Delicious ANTicipation

Wafer biscuits
Icing (page 152) – colour of choice
Chocolate-coated peanuts of varying sizes
Banana-shaped sweets
Coloured balls
Hundreds and thousands

1. Coat the wafer biscuits with a layer of icing.
2. Place three chocolate-coated peanuts in position (a small one for the head, a small one for the thorax, and a long one for the abdomen). Attach six banana-shaped sweets to the thorax section with icing to make the legs.
3. Attach the coloured balls to the head section to make the eyes.
4. Sprinkle with hundreds and thousands.

Beautiful butterflies

Easy Biscuits (page 152)
Icing (page 152) – colour of choice
Small gummy sweets
Silver balls
Small round sweets
Banana-shaped sweets
Liquorice strips
Edible glitter

1. Prepare the biscuit dough as per the recipe, and use a butterfly-shaped cookie cutter to cut out the biscuits. Bake as directed and cool completely.
2. Coat the biscuits with a layer of icing.
3. Place a gummy sweet in position for the head, silver balls for eyes and wings, small round sweets for wing spots, banana-shaped sweets for body segments, and liquorice strips for antennae.
4. Dust with a fine sprinkling of edible glitter.

Creepy, creepy crawlies

Edible (wafer) cookie cups
Liquorice Allsorts Mini™
Icing (page 152) – colour of choice
Toothpicks
Ice cream
Sour worm-shaped sweets
Plastic spoons
Silver plastic charms
Craft glue

1. Assemble the head by securing the eyes (Liquorice Allsorts Mini™) to the cookie cup with icing.
2. Attach Liquorice Allsorts Mini™ to toothpicks and insert into the cookie cup to make the antennae.
3. Scoop ice cream onto a plate, position eight legs (sour worms) and top with the cookie cup head.
4. Serve with a plastic spoon to which you have attached a silver plastic charm using craft glue.

AN INSECT'S DELIGHT CAKE

1 x Basic Cake (page 152) – two x 200 mm round cakes
Large dome-shaped sugared jelly sweets
Star-shaped sweets with a hole in the centre
Toothpicks
Icing (page 152) – chocolate, green
2 x 125 g packets of boudoir biscuits
A few white mini marshmallows
A few chocolate-coated peanuts
A few Astros™ or Skittles™
Plastic bugs and butterflies
Wooden skewers
Plastic trees
Broad ribbon, about 750 x 60 mm
Small piece of tape

1. Bake the cakes as per the recipe and allow to cool completely.
2. Insert the dome-shaped sweets through the hole in the centre of the star-shaped sweets to form pretty flowers.
3. Insert toothpicks to form the stems.
4. Coat one of the cake layers with chocolate icing and place on top of the second layer, pressing down slightly to secure.
5. Coat the greater part of the top of the cake with chocolate icing (use the star nozzle if preferred), and the remaining portion with green icing, to create a small lawn area in the garden.
6. Coat the sides of the cake with chocolate icing and attach the boudoir biscuits with the smooth side facing in to create a fence.
7. Cut slices from the broader part of the marshmallows and use as the paving stones.
8. Insert the flowers into the cake on the one side of the paving stones, varying the height of the flowers.
9. Create two piles of 'rocks' using the chocolate-coated peanuts and the Astros™ or Skittles™.
10. Attach the flying insects to wooden skewers that have been cut to size and insert them into the cake, again varying their heights.
11. Position the rest of the insects and trees as desired.
12. Lastly tie a broad ribbon around the outside of the cake to neaten the appearance of the biscuits, overlapping the ends and securing with a piece of tape. If you don't have a ribbon that is sufficiently broad, cut a length of crepe paper to size and tie the ribbon around that.

Allocate more time to the duration of this party (or simply visit fewer countries!), as there are a lot of activities. After the initial planning it really is quite simple, and a great deal of fun.

Around the

SETTING THE SCENE

★ Choose five destinations and create posters to decorate the various stops, identifying each country with a famous landmark or feature.

★ Arrange enough seats for all the children in two rows, one behind the other, with an aisle in between, as found on an aeroplane. An adult acts as the tour guide.

★ Tie white balloons in bundles and suspend from the trees, or the ceiling if the party is indoors, to resemble clouds.

★ Position a table and chair at the entrance, signposted 'Passport Control'. As the children arrive, paste the photos they have been asked to bring (see Invitations) into their passports. (Have a few stickers available in case someone has forgotten a photograph.)

★ Have a container marked 'Valuable Goods' where children can deposit the gifts.

★ The children proceed to the 'Boarding Gate' (signposted), where they receive their 'baggage' (treat bags), and are directed to their seats.

★ Set the tone with music such as *I'm leaving on a jet plane*, *Summer holiday*, and so on.

★ Once everyone is seated, the tour guide provides brief information about their destination. Children disembark at their first stop for snacks and games.

Recommended age group: 6–10

World

INVITATIONS

YOU WILL NEED (PER INVITATION):
Coloured notepaper measuring 140 x 140 mm
Pen or pencil
Aeroplane template (page 156) or a sticker of choice
Scissors
Craft glue
Stiff paper measuring 180 x 180 mm

1. Write the party details (*see* Suggested wording) on the coloured notepaper.

2. Trace the image of an aeroplane onto paper using the template provided, or use a sticker of your choice. Cut out and glue it onto the notepaper.

3. To make a folder for the invitation, fold the stiff paper in half.

4. Glue the two sides, but leave the top open, thus creating a neat envelope. Fold the party details in half and slip them into the folder.

5. Use the aeroplane template again to decorate the folder, and include both the guest's and party child's names on the folder.

SUGGESTED WORDING
Thank you for travelling with (birthday child)'s Airline.
Tourist: (guest's name)
Airport: (party address)
Departure date: (date of party)
Departure time: (start of party)
Expected time of arrival: (end of party)
Confirm reservation: travel agent at (phone number) by (date)
Dress: as tourists (wear travel hats, sunglasses, scarves, binoculars, etc.)
Please bring a small photograph of yourself to the party for use on your passport.

TREAT BAGS

Note: These bags must be handed out at the beginning of the party (see page 47).

YOU WILL NEED (PER BAG):
Aeroplane template
(page 156)
Paper of choice
Crayons or
colouring pens
Glitter
Scissors
Craft glue
Brown paper gift bag
with cord handles
Polyester fibre
filling for clouds
Curling ribbons

1. Enlarge the template of the aeroplane to the preferred size, trace it onto paper, colour brightly, decorate with glitter or as preferred, cut out and paste onto the front of the gift bag. Add a few blobs of the fibre filling for surrounding cloud.

2. Attach curling ribbons to the cord handles.

3. Write the guest's name on the 'baggage'.

4. Insert a small packet of crisps, a container of fruit juice and a few sweets for the children to nibble during the 'flight'.

5. Further treats will be collected during the journey.

PASSPORTS

**YOU WILL NEED
(PER PASSPORT):**
Stiff paper measuring
180 x 130 mm
Globe template
(page 156) or a sticker
Gold glitter glue
2 x sheets of paper
measuring
160 x 100 mm
Stapler
Pen or pencil

1. Fold the stiff paper in half and decorate the front using the globe. Use the glitter glue to write 'PASSPORT' above the globe.
2. Fold the other sheets of paper in half and insert them into the cover. Staple neatly along the cover's folded edge to form a booklet.
3. Print the guest's name on the first page. The guest's photograph must be attached as they arrive at the party (remember to have glue handy).
4. Attach stickers at each destination, or use a stamp.
5. The children may take these passports home as a memento and record of their activities.

DESTINATION 1 – ENGLAND

PARTY FOOD
Coronation jellies

Jelly (powder or cubes)
Transparent plastic serving tubs
Hundreds and thousands
Plastic spoons
Silver plastic charms
Craft glue

1. Prepare the jelly according to package instructions using flavour of choice (pineapple best signifies gold) and pour into transparent plastic tubs.
2. Allow to set partially, then add a sprinkling of hundreds and thousands.
3. Leave in the fridge to set completely.
4. Attach a plastic charm to the spoon with the craft glue. The children may take these home.

GAME
Pass the crown

YOU WILL NEED:
Toy crown or coronet
Music

The children must sit in a circle and pass the crown from one to the other while the music plays. When the music stops the child holding the crown is eliminated.

The game continues to the last remaining child, who is the winner and receives a small prize plus a sticker associated with the particular country.

The rest of the children receive a sticker for their passports (have a helper attach the stickers as the children are eliminated from the game).

After this stop has been completed, the children return to the 'aeroplane' where they are briefed about their next destination.

DESTINATION 2 – FRANCE

PARTY FOOD
French ladies

Sweetie Pies® or Tunnock's Tea Cakes™
Marie biscuits or Rich Tea™ biscuits
Icing (page 152) – colour of choice
Small dolls
Silver balls

1. Attach a Sweetie Pie® or tea cake to a Marie or tea biscuit with icing.
2. Make an incision in the top of the Sweetie Pie® or tea cake with a knife. Work carefully as the chocolate is fragile.
3. Insert a small doll so that the chocolate forms a skirt.
4. Using a star nozzle, cover the skirt and doll's bodice with icing.
5. Attach silver ball 'buttons' to the bodice and pipe two stars to form a hat.
6. Use a different colour icing for each doll.

GAME
Parisian fashion

YOU WILL NEED:
Dressing up clothes and accessories

Place bundles of dressing up clothes and accessories in a circle, ensuring that there are sufficient bundles for the number of children. You may include necklaces, ties, hats, shoes, wigs, etc. Predetermine how many items you will have in each bundle as it will affect the length of the game.

While the music plays, the children skip around the circle. When the music stops, they have to don one item from the bundle beside them. The game ends when all the clothes have been used. Prizes may be awarded for: Most Elegant Lady, Debonair Gentleman, and so on.

Attach the stickers for this destination to the passports. Return to the 'aeroplane' to 'fly' to the next destination.

DESTINATION 3 – SOUTH AFRICA

PARTY FOOD
Big Five juice

Juices of choice
Animal ice cubes (small plastic animals inserted into the ice tray when freezing the ice cubes)

Note: The animal ice cubes form the basis of the game.

GAME
Wild animal walk

Each child has a turn to tell the group which animal he/she has found in their ice cube, and must mimic the noise and gait. The children get to choose the best performance for the prize. All keep their animals.

Attach the stickers for this destination to the passports. Return to the 'aeroplane' to 'fly' to the next destination.

DESTINATION 4 – EGYPT

PARTY FOOD
Mummy biscuits

Easy Biscuits (page 153)
Gingerbread man cookie cutter
Icing (page 152) – white
Silver or gold balls

1. Prepare the biscuit dough as per the recipe. The dough is sufficient for about 15 large mummies.
2. Cut out the biscuits with the cookie cutter and bake as directed.
3. When cool, pipe on the bandages using a ribbon nozzle and the white icing.
4. Place two silver or gold balls on the face for eyes.

GAME
Mummy wrap

YOU WILL NEED:
Toilet rolls

Divide the children into groups of four or five and give each group two toilet rolls.

The groups choose a candidate to be wrapped up like a mummy – faces must be kept open – and are allocated a time to do this. The children choose the best mummy and the winning group receives a prize.

Attach the stickers for this destination to the passports. Return to the 'aeroplane' to 'fly' to the next destination.

DESTINATION 5 – CHINA

PARTY FOOD AND GAME
Chopstick marshmallows

Set of chopsticks for each child
(disposable ones are best)
Mini marshmallows

Set out a few bowls of mini marshmallows on a table and provide each child with a set of chopsticks.

A timer is set (an egg timer is ideal) and the children compete to pick up the most marshmallows using the chopsticks. The winner receives a prize and all the children get to keep their chopsticks.

This marks the end of the journey. The tour operator thanks the children and then proceeds to cut the birthday cake.

BON VOYAGE CAKE

1 x Basic Cake (page 152)
– 330 x 260 mm
Sugar paste, coloured grey
Cut white strips from
Liquorice Allsorts™
Icing (page 152) – green
Wafer biscuit
2 x toy aeroplanes
Candy sticks
Sweets of choice
Polyester fibre filling
attached to florist's wire
Selection of toys

1. Bake the cake as directed and leave to cool completely.
2. Mark out the runway section on the cake. Roll out the sugar paste for the runway and cut to fit the designated section. Lay it on the cake and attach the white strips of Liquorice Allsorts™ for the centre markings.
3. Using a star nozzle, ice the surrounds as illustrated.
4. Secure a wafer biscuit wedge onto one edge of the runway strip with icing and rest a toy plane against it in a 'take off' position. Place the other toy plane at the other end of the runway.
5. Position the candy sticks and sweets for the light posts and runway edging.
6. Wrap a small piece of aluminium foil around the section of the florist's wire that will be submerged in the cake, and place in position with the fibre filling attached (keep the candles away from the clouds).
7. Decorate the surrounds of the cake with additional toys as desired.

This is a popular theme with children of this age group, and aspirations of becoming an astronaut may well be entertained during this birthday celebration!

Spectacular

SETTING THE SCENE

* Suspend bundles of polyester filling in the doorway so that the children may 'pass through the earth's atmosphere' as they enter the party room.

* Line the walls with black crepe paper or cloth or use silver foil and attach stars and moons made from construction paper and painted gold or silver.

* Add white Christmas lights to twinkle as stars.

* Use fishing line to suspend stars and moons from the ceiling – these may be made from construction paper, painted in bright colours and decorated with glitter. (If the party is held in the early evening, glow-in-the-dark items are effective.)

* Include bundles of 'clouds'.

* Make planets from Styrofoam balls that have been sprayed gold or silver and hang them from the ceiling – wrap silver tinsel around the circumference of a few of the planets.

* Cover the party table with aluminium foil or silver crepe paper and sprinkle with confetti moons and stars.

* Spray a few pebbles with silver spray and use these 'moon rocks' to decorate the table.

Recommended age group: 4–8

Space

INVITATIONS

YOU WILL NEED:

Plastic spheres (readily available from plastic wholesale stores)
Gold and/or silver self-adhesive stars
Notepaper
Pen or pencil
Small toy spacemen, or sweets if preferred
Curling ribbon (optional)

1. Decorate the plastic spheres with the stars.
2. Write the invitation details (*see* Suggested wording) on the notepaper, fold and place inside the sphere together with a small space toy or some sweets.
3. If using the curling ribbon, hook it around one of the sphere prongs, before assembly, then fasten the two halves of the sphere together. Knot the ends of the ribbon together.

SUGGESTED WORDING

Orbit the earth at (birthday child's name)'s party.
Mission control: (address)
Blast off: (date and time the party starts)
Touch down: (party ends)
RSVP: mission commander at (phone number) by (date)

TREAT BAGS

YOU WILL NEED (PER BAG):

8–10 strips of crepe paper, about 250 mm long x 20 mm wide
Glitter glue
1 x disposable party plate
Stiff white card
Prestik® or Blu-tac™
2 x 60 mm lengths of pipe cleaner
Felt-tip marker
1 x disposable cake dome to fit plate
Craft glue
Self-adhesive stars

1. Apply a thin layer of glitter glue to each strip of crepe paper and allow to dry before attaching to the underside of the plate, along the bottom edge, ensuring that the glitter-coated surface faces up. This forms the 'vapour trail'.
2. Cut a circle from the card, measuring about 60 mm in diameter, place a small ball of Prestik® or Blu-tac™ in the centre and attach the two pipe cleaners, so that they stand upright in the shape of a V to form the antennae.
3. Write the guest's name on the circle of card with the felt-tip marker, decorate with glitter glue and attach to the centre of the upturned cake dome with craft glue.
4. Attach the adhesive stars to the dome and place the dome over the plate.

GAMES AND ACTIVITIES

The star trail

YOU WILL NEED:
Cardboard stars, sufficient for each child
Small token for each child

Hide the cardboard stars throughout the garden or house and instruct the children to find them. After each child has found a star, they may pair up to help the rest, until each child has a star.

Each star should be numbered to correspond with a token (numbered accordingly).

Rocket booster race

YOU WILL NEED:
1 x large cardboard box for each team
Balloons (a few more than the number of children)

Divide the children into two or more teams and provide each team with a cardboard box from which you have removed the top and bottom.

On starter's orders, the first child in each team steps into the box and races to a designated spot where you have hung bunches of balloons.

The child steps out of the box, takes a balloon (an adult can help here), sits on it to pop it, gets back into the 'rocket' and returns to 'earth'. The next child gets into the rocket and the game continues until all have popped a balloon. The first team to finish wins a prize, the rest receive tokens.

Touch down

YOU WILL NEED:
Hula Hoop
Frisbee

Place a Hula Hoop on the ground, or mark a circle if you prefer. Draw a 'launching' line about two metres away from the hoop. The children must toss a flying saucer (frisbee) to land in the circle.

Once each child has had a turn – those who miss the circle are eliminated – the mark is moved further away, about half a metre each time. The game continues until there is a winner.

Three-legged aliens

YOU WILL NEED:
Cord for tying children's ankles together
Material for blindfolds for each pair

Divide the children into pairs. One leg of each child is tied together with a suitable length of cord and one of the pair is blindfolded.

Start and finish lines are predetermined. On starter's orders, the aliens must race to the finish line, with the blindfolded child being ably assisted by his or her partner. The winners receive a prize while the rest of the children receive a token.

PARTY FOOD

Lift off

Party Cupcakes (page 153)
Icing (page 152) – colour of choice
Silver vermicelli
Flat, round boiled sweets
Large dome-shaped sugared jelly sweets
Liquorice Allsorts™
Star-shaped sweets

1. Bake the cupcakes according to the recipe and allow to cool completely.
2. Coat the top with a layer of icing and sprinkle with silver vermicelli.
3. Use three or four flat, round sweets and attach one on top of the other with a small blob of icing. Place on the cupcake. Position the dome sweet on the top, again using icing to secure.
4. Cut two Liquorice Allsorts™ squares diagonally in half and attach with icing to the base of the rocket.
5. Add star-shaped sweets to enhance the theme.

Milky Way surprise

MAKES ABOUT 20 PORTIONS
4 x packets of jelly, each a different colour
1 litre boiling water
2 x 380 g tins of evaporated milk, chilled
Star-shaped sweets and silver balls

1. Mix the jellies, one at a time. Dissolve the first jelly in 1 cup (250 ml) boiling water. Leave to cool, then fold in half a tin whipped evaporated milk.
2. Pour into a large bowl and refrigerate until set.
3. Mix the second jelly in the same manner and, after folding in the milk, gently pour over the first jelly and allow this to set.
4. Continue the same process with the third, and finally the fourth jelly.
5. Before serving, sprinkle the top with a few star-shaped sweets and silver balls.

Alien ice cream

Googly eyes
Silver pipe cleaners
Wafer ice-cream cones
Ice cream of choice

1. Attach googly eyes to the ends of silver pipe cleaners and wrap around ice-cream cones.
2. Just before serving, top with a scoop of ice cream.

Take me to your leader!

Small sweets of choice
Edible (wafer) cookie cups
Marie biscuits or Rich Tea™ biscuits
Icing (page 152) – colour of choice
Colourful lollipops
Marshmallows
Candy sticks, cut to size
Large silver balls
Liquorice Allsorts™, small and large
Coloured balls

1. Place the small sweets in a wafer cookie cup and use icing to attach a Marie or tea biscuit to cover. Flip over so that the biscuit forms the base.
2. Use a colourful lollipop for the face and push the stick through a marshmallow to make the body.
3. Insert the protruding stick into the top of the cookie cup to create the alien.
4. Use blobs of icing to attach the candy stick eyestalks to the top of the head, as well as those at the waist.
5. Attach the silver balls in the same manner.
6. A small Liquorice Allsorts™, makes up the eye, and a Liquorice Allsorts™ square is attached to the marshmallow to create a 'control panel'. Position the coloured balls for the dials on the panel.
7. Pipe three squiggly legs down the front of the cookie cup.

FLYING SAUCER CAKE

1 x Basic Cake (page 152) – 250 mm round cake

Icing (page 152) – white

Silver dust

Flat round sweets

4 x plastic Martians

4 x Liquorice Allsorts™

Large silver balls

4 x gum balls

Clear plastic bowl, about 125 mm diameter

1 large orange ball sweet

10 x candy sticks covered in foil

Small silver balls

Orange star-shaped sweets

Yellow star-shaped sweets

2 x wafer ice-cream cones, cup section removed and cone section covered with foil

Polyester fibre filling

1. Bake the cake as per the recipe and allow to cool completely.
2. Coat the top and sides of the cake with icing.
3. Brush the top with silver dust.
4. Arrange the flat round sweets around the edge of the cake.
5. Position the four Martians in the centre of the cake and create a control panel in front of each one using a Liquorice Allsorts™ square and a large silver ball.
6. Place a gum ball beside each Martian.
7. Place the plastic bowl over the toys and pipe a swirl of icing on the top of the bowl.
8. Position the orange ball sweet in the icing and attach two candy sticks to create the antennae.
9. Add large silver balls to the ends of the antennae and arrange smaller balls around the outer edge of the icing mound.
10. Using the star nozzle, pipe a small circle of stars around the rim of the bowl and place silver balls on random stars.
11. Arrange orange and yellow star-shaped sweets on the 'body' of the flying saucer.
12. Insert the remaining candy sticks around the side of the cake and attach a large silver ball to the end of each one.
13. Insert half a wooden skewer through each cone and attach to the back end.
14. Add the fibre filling vapour trails to each cone.

It is likely that boys won't want to attend this particular party and this theme may appear to focus on girls, but the ideas can be used and adapted using colours of choice. You may also combine two colours, for example, pink and blue (for the boys) – the possibilities are endless!

SETTING THE SCENE

✳ Tie bundles of pink balloons with pink curling ribbon and place wherever possible, including the garden gate.

✳ Suspend crepe paper streamers in the doorway.

✳ Cover the table with pink crepe paper and top with a piece of ruched pink tulle.

✳ Scatter pink flower petals over the table.

✳ Hang pink crepe paper streamers from the garden trees and shrubs.

✳ Cut shapes, such as stars, hearts and moons, from cardboard, spray with pink craft spray and suspend from the ceiling, trees and shrubs with fishing line.

Recommended age group: 3–10

Pink

INVITATIONS

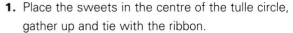

YOU WILL NEED (PER INVITATION):
Circle of pink tulle, about 250 mm in diameter
Dainty pink sweets
Pink curling ribbon
Stiff pink card
Pen
Glitter glue

1. Place the sweets in the centre of the tulle circle, gather up and tie with the ribbon.
2. Write the party details (*see* Suggested wording) on the card, decorate with glitter glue and attach it to the ribbon.

SUGGESTED WORDING
A spell has been cast on (birthday child's name) – on the day of her (age) birthday, everything she touches will turn perfectly pink! Come and join the fun!
The pink house: (address)
The pink day: (party date)
The pink time: (party times)
RSVP: the pink lady at (phone number) by (date)
Dress: pink!

TREAT BAGS

YOU WILL NEED (PER BAG):
Empty, clean 2-litre plastic milk or juice container
Scissors or craft knife
Paper punch
Pink non-toxic craft spray
Flower template (page 156)
Stiff card (use a contrasting colour of choice)
Glitter glue
Craft glue
Pink ribbon, cord or pipe cleaner for the handle
Curling ribbon

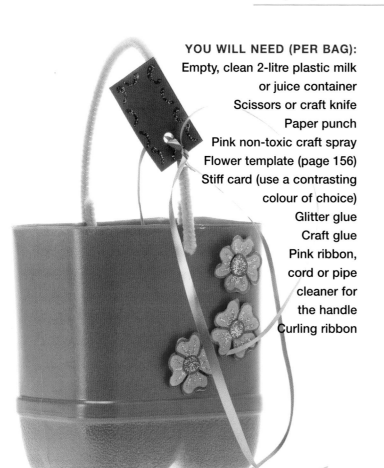

1. Cut the top section from the container, just below the handle, and discard.
2. Use a paper punch to make a hole on either side, near the rim of the container.
3. Spray the container with pink craft spray and allow to dry.
4. Enlarge the template to the preferred size, cut it out and trace three flowers onto the stiff card. Cut out the flowers, decorate with glitter glue and attach to the front of the container with craft glue.
5. Thread the ribbon or cord through the holes and knot the ends to make a handle, or use a pipe cleaner if preferred.
6. Write the guest's name on stiff card and attach it to the handle with curling ribbon.

GAMES AND ACTIVITIES

Rosy fortunes

YOU WILL NEED:
Pink sheets or cloths
Gypsy fancy dress
Artificial crystal ball or playing cards

Drape a corner of the party area with pink sheets or other cloth to create a makeshift tent.

Have an adult or teenage helper, dressed as a gypsy in pink, 'forecast' each child's 'fortune'. The children will be delighted to hear sweet tales.

Pink parcel

YOU WILL NEED:
Small gift
Pink wrapping paper
Black wrapping paper
Music
Pink bag containing forfeits (the forfeits are determined by the age of the children and can be simple, such as: 'Mew like a kitten', 'Recite a nursery rhyme', 'Leap like a frog')

Wrap a small gift in layers of pink paper with a random addition of black wrapping paper layers.

Instruct the children to sit in a circle and, when the music plays, they must pass the parcel from one to the other. When the music stops, the child who has the parcel removes a layer of wrapping.

The child who uncovers a black parcel has to perform a forfeit (chosen from the pink bag). The child who unwraps the last layer of wrapping gets to keep the gift.

Pink surprises

YOU WILL NEED:
Small gift for each child
Pink wrapping paper
Small plastic curtain rings
Cardboard box covered in pink paper and decorated with attached balloons and streamers
Pink paper bag containing a number for each child
Dowel rod, about 250 mm long, sprayed pink and decorated with ribbons, with a cup hook attached to one end

Wrap a small gift for each child in pink paper and attach a plastic curtain ring to each parcel. Place the parcels in the box. (Provide one or two extra so that the last child also has a reasonable choice. The leftover gifts may be used as prizes in other games.)

Instruct the children to draw a number from the pink bag, which determines their place in the queue. Using the magic wand, each child has a turn to hook a gift out of the box.

Pink knobbly knees race

YOU WILL NEED:
Pink balloons

Divide the children into two teams, with the children on each team lined up one behind the other.

On starter's orders, the first child in each team wedges a balloon between her knees and runs to a designated line and back. The balloon is handed to the next child and the procedure continues until all the children have had a turn.

If the balloon slips out, the child has to stop and put it back before continuing. However, should the balloon pop, that particular child has to return to the starting point and re-run the race with another balloon.

The winning team receives a prize, while the remaining children receive a small token.

PARTY FOOD

Shimmering hearts

Party Cupcakes (page 153)
Silver cookie cups (muffin cases)
Icing (page 152) – pink, white
Pink or silver heart-shaped sweets
Silver or pink balls

1. Bake the cupcakes in the silver cookie cups as per the recipe and allow to cool completely.
2. Use the star nozzle to pipe alternating pink and white circles. Place one or two heart sweets in the centre and add silver or pink balls.

Pink ladies with parasols

Wafer ice-cream cones
Sweets of choice
Marie biscuits or Rich Tea™ biscuits
Icing (page 152) – yellow, pink
White marshmallows
White pipe cleaners (about 60 mm long)
Pink paper parasols
Pink star-shaped sweets
Silver balls

1. Fill a wafer cone with sweets.
2. Coat a Marie or tea biscuit with icing and place over the open end of the cone. Upend so that the biscuit forms the base. Snip the tip off and discard.
3. Coat the open end of the cone with icing, as well as one side of a marshmallow, and place the marshmallow on the cone to make the lady's head.
4. Cut a pipe cleaner in half and insert it through the sides of the cone as illustrated, to resemble the arms.
5. Use yellow icing to pipe strands of hair.
6. Gently insert the parasol through the marshmallow to provide additional support to the head.
7. Place a small star-shaped sweet in the hair.
8. Use food colouring or icing to add facial features.
9. Decorate the rest of the cone as illustrated.

Pink jelly

MAKES ABOUT 8 PORTIONS

1 x packet strawberry or cherry jelly (powder or cubes)
1 cup (250 ml) boiling water
⅔ cup (160 ml) condensed milk
Mould of choice

1. Dissolve the jelly in the boiling water.
2. Allow to cool before stirring in the condensed milk.
3. Pour the mixture into a jelly mould and allow to set in the fridge for 2–3 hours.

Pleasantly pink crabsticks

Large polystyrene ball
Pink non-toxic craft spray
2 x pink pipe cleaners
Craft glue
2 x googly eyes
Crabsticks
Pink mayonnaise (2 Tbsp (30 ml) tomato sauce,
   1 cup (250 ml) mayonnaise, a dash of lemon juice)

1. Cut the ball in half and spray with pink craft spray. Place one half, cut side down, on a serving platter.
2. Insert two pipe cleaners to resemble antennae, curling the ends slightly. Use craft glue to attach the googly eyes to the front of the creature.
3. Cut the crabsticks into slices and skewer onto frilly toothpicks. Stick them into the body.
4. Serve the pink mayonnaise on the side.

Other food ideas

Posh meringues: piped nests of pink meringue filled with sliced strawberries. Top with whipped cream.
Pastel pink milkshakes
Pink candy floss

PINK CADILLAC CAKE

1 x Basic Cake (page 152) – 330 x 260 mm

Icing (page 152) – pink, yellow

2 x wafer biscuits

Doll of choice

1 x round Liquorice Allsorts™

Transparent strip (about 12 cm long x 5.5 cm wide) cut from 2-litre plastic bottle

1 x yellow star-shaped sweet

Small silver balls

2 x round sugared jelly sweets

2 x striped marshmallow twists

4 x Oreo® biscuits

4 x large silver balls

1 x foil-covered candy stick

2 x orange and 2 x red gummy dome-shaped sweets

2 x pieces liquorice

3 x small banana-shaped sweets

2 x yellow gummy dome-shaped sweets

1. Bake the cake according to the recipe and allow to cool completely.
2. Cut the cake in half across the width.
3. Remove a 40 x 60 mm section from the middle of one half of the cake to allow space for the doll.
4. Sandwich the two halves together with a layer of icing.
5. Insert one wafer biscuit into the back of the space to provide the back of the seat with a head rest. Use the remaining wafer biscuit, cut to size, to line the sides of the space.
6. Use a sharp knife to slice thin pieces of cake off the front 'bonnet' section, rounding the edge slightly to create the shape of the car.
7. Coat the entire cake with pink icing.
8. Remove the doll's legs and insert the body section into the cake.
9. Attach the round Liquorice Allsorts™ (steering wheel) to the 'dashboard'.
10. Position the windscreen (plastic strip) and use the star nozzle to pipe a delicate row of pink stars around the edges to define it.
11. Pipe pink stars to define the doors, the back boot and along the back upper edge.
12. Pipe two rows of yellow stars down the bonnet and attach the star-shaped sweet (emblem) to the bonnet.
13. Use the silver balls to define the grille and attach the round jelly sweets to create the headlights.
14. Attach the two striped marshmallow twists for the front and back bumpers.
15. Coat one side of each Oreo® with a layer of icing and place in position for the wheels. Pipe on a hubcap and add a big silver ball to the centre to adorn each wheel.
16. Place the candy stick (aerial) in position and add the orange and red dome-shaped sweets for the tail lights.
17. Insert the pieces of liquorice for the twin exhaust.
18. Add the small banana-shaped sweets for door handles and the rear boot handle.
19. Attach the yellow dome-shaped sweets for the side mirrors.
20. For a boy's party, the colours can be changed accordingly with a dashing male doll driving the car instead.

SETTING THE SCENE

* Toy stores always have an abundance of toy wild animals in all shapes and sizes, so party favours and props for this party are easy to find.

* Taped recordings of animal sounds will add to the excitement of the safari party if played as the children arrive.

* Use an abundance of green balloons, with streamers suspended from the ceiling.

* Drape ivy vines from the ceiling and hang in the doorway.

* Place large pot plants at the entrance. A large coiled toy snake peeping from behind the pot plants and perhaps a giant lizard lazing on a rock from the garden are guaranteed to cause a ripple of excitement among the children as they arrive.

* Draw monkeys on poster paper and hang them from the vines.

* If possible, use large foliage (giant strelitzia or palms work well) from the garden and arrange strategically to add to the jungle atmosphere.

* Draw or stencil various animal paw prints onto a sheet of brown paper and use these to cover the party table. Top with a sheet of clear plastic and arrange small pot plants and other greenery on the table. Scatter plastic wild animals between the greenery.

* Arrange toy snakes in the garden and hang paper monkeys and birds from the trees.

Recommended age group: 4-10

Safari

INVITATIONS

YOU WILL NEED (PER INVITATION):
Lion template (page 155)
Pen or pencil
Craft knife and scissors
Orange construction paper
Second sheet of construction paper, a shade lighter than the one above
2 x googly eyes
Craft glue
Fishing line for whiskers, cut to size
Masking tape
Black felt
Felt-tip marker
Red notepaper measuring 95 mm wide x 70 mm long
Prestik® or Blu-tac™

1. Enlarge the template to the preferred size, cut it out and trace the mane outline onto the piece of orange construction paper. Cut out.
2. Trace the face onto the paler paper. Cut out.
3. Glue the googly eyes in position.
4. Push fishing line through the paper for the whiskers, tying a knot or securing with masking tape.
5. Cut a triangle from the black felt and glue it to the face to make the nose. Draw the remaining features with the felt-tip marker.
6. Using a craft knife, make a slit along the outline of the upper lip, leaving 20 mm intact on either side.
7. Write the details (*see* Suggested wording) on the red paper. Fold it into three along the width. Trim one end to shape the tongue – do not cut into the details. Insert the tongue into the slit in the mouth so that half of it protrudes. Secure with a piece of Prestik® or Blu-tac™ that will 'give' when tugged.
8. Apply glue to the back, outer edge of the face, not the tongue area, and attach it to the mane.

SUGGESTED WORDING
Follow the roar of the lion to (child's name)'s party.
Safari park: (address)
Game drive: (date and times of party)
RSVP: game ranger at (phone number) by (date)
Dress: as for a safari

TREAT BAGS

YOU WILL NEED:
Lion template (page 155) and same materials as the invitations
Brown paper bags
Wooden clothes pegs

1. Use the same template as for the invitations, but don't enlarge it too much.
2. Decorate as per steps 1–5 above, omitting the pull-out tongue. Glue the face onto the mane section.
3. Glue the lion face to a wooden clothes peg.
4. Fold over the upper edge of the paper bag and attach the clothes peg.

GAMES AND ACTIVITIES

Game spotting drive

YOU WILL NEED:
Plastic toy animals
A length of rope for each group
Hand-drawn maps, containing clues, for each group

Colour-code and number the plastic animals (one for each child) and hide them in the garden before the children arrive.

Divide the children into groups and give each group a colour. Tie the children in each group together by means of a long rope knotted loosely round their waists, so that each group has a 'safari vehicle'.

Together with the colour, each child receives a number that will determine their prize – the hidden animals are numbered accordingly. Each group receives their own colour-coded map and must follow the clues to find the animals.

There should be a few obstacles along the way (this will vary depending on the children's age and agility), such as 'snake pits', 'rapids to cross', 'poachers' traps', and so on.

Huff and puff

YOU WILL NEED:
A feather for each group

Divide the children into groups and give each group a feather. (You may give more than one feather to each group to add to the fun!) On starter's orders, the groups have to keep the feathers in the air by blowing at them.

The group that keeps the feather/s aloft for the longest time is awarded a prize, the rest receive smaller tokens.

Baby elephant walk

YOU WILL NEED:
Peanuts in the shell
2 x elephant trunks – stuff a leg of pantyhose with fibre filling and attach an elastic cord to fit around a child's head
2 x elephant tails – make a smaller version of the trunk, replacing the elastic with a safety pin, to attach to a child's clothes
2 x small plastic buckets

Determine a starting point as well as an end point and lay two trails of peanuts between the two.

Divide the children into two teams, lined up in a row. The front child of each row wears a 'trunk' and the end child has a 'tail' pinned on.

The children must bend down and reach through the legs of the child in front of them to hold their hand, while simultaneously holding the hand of the person behind them, who is doing the same.

On starter's orders, they must follow the trail while making their best elephant noises. The child in front has to scoop the peanuts into a bucket – the first team to finish with the correct amount of peanuts wins a prize, the rest receive smaller tokens.

Snake leap

YOU WILL NEED:
2 x plastic/rubber toy snakes

Position the snakes along the ground, parallel to each other, about 300 mm apart.

Instruct the children to stand in a line and take turns to jump over the snakes. At the end of each round, move one of the snakes further away by about 200 mm. Continue in this manner, gradually widening the gap, until the children are eliminated and a winner remains.

PARTY FOOD

Swampy serpents

The birthday child can prepare these!

Clean, sterile needle and thread
Jelly Tots™
Large dome-shaped sugared jelly sweets
Silver balls
Liquorice strips (cut a forked shape at one end)
Icing (page 152) – colour of choice

1. Use the needle and thread to make a string of Jelly Tots™, with the larger sweet as the head.
2. Attach the eyes (silver balls) and the forked liquorice tongue with a little dab of icing.

Hungry lion cupcakes

Party Cupcakes (page 153)
Icing (page 152) – yellow, chocolate, red
Gold or silver balls for the eyes

1. Bake the cupcakes as per the recipe and allow to cool completely.
2. Coat the top of the cupcakes with yellow icing.
3. Using the star nozzle and chocolate icing, pull out the icing to create a mane.
4. Attach the eyes to stars of icing and pipe on the mouth. If preferred, use a red sweet for the tongue.

African gold soil

Chocolate Crispies (page 153)
Edible gold dust

1. Make a batch of chocolate crispies as per the recipe and allow to set in the fridge.
2. Sprinkle with gold dust and keep refrigerated until serving.

Endangered species pies

Sausage Pie filling (page 154)
Ready-made frozen puff pastry
Animal-shaped cookie cutters
Tomato sauce and/or mustard

1. Prepare the sausage pie filling as per the recipe.
2. Defrost the pastry and roll out to 4–5 mm thick.
3. Use animal-shaped cookie cutters to cut out pairs of animal shapes. Each pair will form a pie.
4. Fill the pies, seal, and bake as directed.
5. Serve warm with tomato sauce and/or mustard.

Bush thrashers

Wafer biscuits
Icing (page 152) – colour of choice
Round sweets
Liquorice Allsorts™
Jelly Babies™
Worm-shaped jelly sweets
Jelly Tots™

1. Sandwich two wafer biscuits together with icing and coat with dark green, olive or brown icing to resemble a four-wheel drive vehicle.
2. Using dabs of icing, attach five round sweets – four wheels and one spare.
3. Position the Liquorice Allsorts™ to make the seats.
4. Place two Jelly Babies™ in position on the liquorice seats.
5. Place a halved jelly worm for the windshield and the Jelly Tots™ in front for the headlights.

Other food ideas

Campers in sleeping bags: wrap asparagus spears in slices of ham and serve on a bed of shredded lettuce.

JUNGLE CAKE

1 x Basic Cake (page 152) – 330 x 260 mm

Icing (page 152) – chocolate, green, green-brown, light brown

About 2 Marie biscuits or Rich Tea™ biscuits, crumbled

A little cocoa powder

Desiccated coconut, coloured green

Two or three chocolate crispies (reserved from the African Gold Soil recipe, page 74)

6 x Oreo® biscuits

2 x circles cut from stiff card, about 60 mm in diameter – cut a slit along the radius and
   fold one section over the other to create a pitched roof (secure with a staple)

1 x small Flake® chocolate

Small, narrow strip cut from a 2-litre plastic bottle

Large dome-shaped sugared jelly sweets

Jelly Tots™

Toothpicks

Small plastic animals and trees

Small toy cars

1. Bake the cake according to the recipe and allow to cool completely.

2. Using a sharp knife, mark out the different sections on the cake – the road, the camp site,
   the grassed sections and the watering hole.

3. Start with the roadway: use light brown icing and cover the road with Marie or tea biscuit
   crumbs that have been lightly mixed with cocoa powder.

4. If preferred, use a star nozzle and green icing for the grassed areas and sprinkle with the green
   desiccated coconut.

5. Scoop out a shallow layer of cake to 'sink' the watering hole, then ice the surroundings with
   chocolate icing. Use a blue-green shade of icing for the water. Crumble the chocolate crispies
   and arrange around the watering hole.

6. To make the bungalows, pile three Oreo® biscuits on top of each other, securing with
   a thin layer of icing between each.

7. Coat the bungalow roofs with brown icing and place on top of the Oreos®.

8. Cover with Flake® chocolate to resemble thatch.

9. Coat the plastic strip with light brown icing and position across the road to make a bridge.

10. Fashion flowers from domed jelly sweets and Jelly Tots™ and skewer with a toothpick.
    Position as desired.

11. Arrange the toys as shown.

The clown template is carried throughout this party for the invitations, treat bags and posters. Young children may be accompanied by their parents, so you will need to cater for them too. In return, they will probably be happy to assist with the activities, but confirm this in advance.

Fun at the

SETTING THE SCENE

* Set up a ticket booth at the entrance: cover a table or bench with a flat sheet or any other large cloth and decorate with balloons and ribbons. Provide background circus music.

  - The children should be welcomed here, may have their faces painted, and be presented with their treat bags.

  - The booth may be manned by an adult dressed as a clown. If you can't manage to put together an entire outfit, a large red plastic nose and a coloured curly wig will suffice. Note, however, that sometimes very young children may be wary of clowns!

* Drape plastic sheets in the doorway and decorate the room with red, white and orange crepe paper streamers draped from the centre of the ceiling to form a tent.

* Use cardboard paper roller towel holders, covered with coloured paper or sprayed with craft spray, and coloured string to make trapezes. Attach teddies or other available toys to the trapezes and suspend from the ceiling with fishing line.

* Set up various booths where children need to queue to 'buy' their party snacks, in true circus style, exchanging their tickets (page 80) for the food. Decorate these booths in the same manner as the ticket booth.

Recommended age group: 3–6

Circus

INVITATIONS

YOU WILL NEED (PER INVITATION):
Clown template (page 155)
Stiff white card measuring
160 x 200 mm
Scissors
Notepaper in different
bright colours
Craft glue
2 x large
googly eyes
1 x red pompom
2 x coloured
pompoms
Sequins and glitter
Lollipop
Masking tape
Ribbon

1. Enlarge the template to the preferred size and trace it onto the stiff white card. Cut out.
2. Use the coloured paper to cut out the hat, lips, cheek spots, hair and bow tie. Glue in position.
3. Decorate the rest of the clown as follows: attach the googly eyes, the red pompom for the nose, the coloured pompoms for the hat, and the sequins and glitter on the bow tie. Attach a lollipop to the hat, securing it at the back with masking tape.
4. Write the party details (*see* Suggested wording) on brightly coloured notepaper to resemble a ticket. Attach to the lollipop using the ribbon.

SUGGESTED WORDING
Free admission to (guest's name) to a circus party!
Star performer: (birthday child's name)
Big top: (address)
Performance time: (date and start and end times)
RSVP: the ringmaster at (phone number) by (date)
Dress: as a clown or circus performer

TREAT BAGS

Note: These bags must be handed out at the beginning of the party.

YOU WILL NEED:
Clown template
(page 155) and
same materials
as for invitations
Brightly coloured
gift bags with
cord handles
Stiff card
Curling ribbon

1. Follow steps 1–3 of the invitation to make the clown. Glue it to the gift bag.
2. Write each guest's name on a card and attach it to the bag's handle with the curling ribbon.

Food tickets

YOU WILL NEED (PER TICKET):
Stiff coloured card measuring about 80 x 40 mm
Felt-tip marker

Cut the card to size and write the party fare on the front, for example 'HOT DOG' or 'POPCORN'. You may need a drawing so that the younger children can easily identify the cards. Place the 'tickets' inside the bag.

GAMES AND ACTIVITIES

You may wish to hire a clown or magician to entertain the children – consult the local newspapers for details and book in advance to avoid disappointment. Give the children a chance to 'purchase' refreshments from the food booths between each activity.

Apart from the organized games given below, Hula Hoops and juggling rings will provide much fun during free play intervals.

Feed the hungry clown

YOU WILL NEED:
Large piece of cardboard
Poster paints
3 x tennis balls

Draw a clown's face onto the cardboard (use the template if preferred). Cut out a large round mouth and paint the poster in primary colours.

The children must stand behind a line – placed a fair distance (depending on age) from the target – and take turns to throw the tennis balls through the mouth.

Each child has to throw three balls and is able to choose a prize once all three balls have reached their target. If necessary, the distance from the target can be reduced until all the children are successful.

Tricky tightrope

YOU WILL NEED:
Length of rope
Toy umbrella

Lay the rope on the ground in a straight line.

One at a time, spin each child around two or three times, then let him or her walk the tightrope with a small umbrella for balance.

The successful acrobats receive a prize, the rest of the children receive smaller tokens.

Speedy clown race

YOU WILL NEED:
2 x clown wigs
2 x clown noses
2 pairs of the biggest shoes available

Group the children into two teams and stand them in line, one behind the other. The front child in each team wears a clown wig, a big red clown nose and a pair of big, big shoes.

On starter's orders, the front child in each team races to a designated spot and back, removes their props and hands them to the next child in line, who repeats the procedure. The activity continues until all the children have had a turn.

The winning team receives a small gift, the remaining children receive a smaller token.

Jump the hoop

YOU WILL NEED:
Hula Hoop
Music

Get the children to stand in a wide circle.

The first child holds a Hula Hoop above his head and when the music starts he must pass the hoop over his body, step out of it and hand it to the next child.

When the music stops the child holding the hoop is out. The game continues until there is a winner.

PARTY FOOD

Clown in a ruff

Party Cupcakes (page 153)
Icing (page 152) – colour of choice
Round sweets
Banana-shaped sweets
Large dome-shaped sugared jelly sweets
Small round sweets
Red banana-shaped sweet

1. Bake the cupcakes according to the recipe, leave to cool completely, then coat with icing.
2. Place a round sweet in the centre and position the banana-shaped sweets to form a ruff.
3. Add the dome-shaped sweet for the hat (secure with a little icing) and use the star nozzle to pipe icing around it, as well as two little stars.
4. Decorate as illustrated.

Cocktail clown

Polystyrene board
Toothpicks
Green and red cocktail onions
Cherry tomatoes
Cocktail sausages
Cheese cubes
Chipniks®, Quavers™ or similar snack

1. Enlarge the clown template (page 155) to the preferred size and trace the outline onto polystyrene board. Cut out the clown shape around the edges.
2. Skewer the food on toothpicks and arrange as follows, grouped closely together:
   Eyes: green cocktail onions
   Nose: cherry tomatoes
   Mouth: red cocktail onions
   Hair: cocktail sausages
   Hat: cheese cubes with cherry tomatoes strategically placed for pompoms
   Bow tie: Chipniks®, Quavers™ or similar snack

Balancing act

Sugar paste, coloured grey
Silver balls
Gum balls
Icing (page 152) – colours of choice
Edible (wafer) cookie cups
Small sweets of choice
Marie biscuits or Rich Tea™ biscuits

1. Knead the sugar paste until smooth. Mould a small walnut-sized ball of the paste into a U shape.
2. At one end of the U, mould a pointed nose. Split the other end into two to create the flipper.
3. Use small blobs of sugar paste to make the side fins, and attach them to the body.
4. Place the silver balls in position for the eyes and secure the gum ball to the tip of the nose with a dot of icing.
5. Place in the fridge to set while preparing the base.
6. Fill the cookie cups with the small sweets.
7. Place a Marie or tea biscuit on top and secure with icing.
8. Upend the cone so that the Marie or tea biscuit forms the base and use the star nozzle and two bright colours to decorate as illustrated.
9. Attach the seal before the icing sets.

Other food ideas

Popcorn: in colourful cardboard containers (available at party supply stores) or plain brown paper packets.
Carbonated cold drinks
Iced lollies
Mini hot dogs: use cocktail sausages and mini rolls and serve with tomato sauce or mustard.

CLOWN CAKE

2 x Basic Cake (page 152) – 330 mm x 260 mm cake, 250 mm round cake

Icing (page 152) – white, red

Half a plastic sphere covered with aluminium foil (to facilitate icing) for the nose

Round, flat, brightly coloured sweets for the hat and the ruff

Large silver balls to enhance the ruff

4 x fruit slice sweets for the eyes – two slices are placed, facing each other, with the rounded edges on the outside

2 x large round sugared jelly sweets for the centre of the eyes (attach large silver balls for the pupils)

2 x large round red sugared jelly sweets for the cheeks

2 x liquorice strips for the eyebrows

About 8 Cheese Curls™ for the hair

Plastic toy balloons for the hat (available at baking/party supply stores)

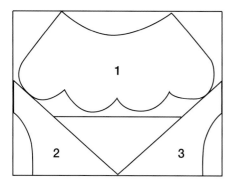

1. Bake the cakes as per the recipe and allow to cool completely. The round cake is obviously used for the face. The ruff and hat are cut from the rectangular cake as shown in the cutting layout above (unfortunately there are off-cuts here), with sections 2 and 3 being placed together for the hat.
2. Join all the sections together and coat the entire cake with white icing.
3. Use a star nozzle to pipe around the edges of the ruff to define the scallops, as well as around the edge of the hat.
4. Coat the plastic half-sphere with red icing and place in position for the nose.
5. Use a toothpick to trace the outline of the mouth then, using the star nozzle, define it with red icing. Ice a centre strip of white to separate the lips.
6. Affix the sweets as illustrated and finish by placing the silver balls in position.

SETTING THE SCENE

- For this party the ideal is to take the children to a nearby field, or to hire a club or school's field. Girls usually enjoy this sort of party just as much as the boys.

- Have a football for children to sign as they arrive, as a memento for the birthday child.

- Cover the party table with dark green crepe paper or cloth and use white tape to create all the appropriate markings of a football field, for example goal lines, centre mark, and so on.

- The party fare may be enjoyed at home after the game, but it will be advisable to serve the Penalty Punch (page 89) at 'half time'.

- An adult, preferably with an assistant, should act as the referee and, of course, a whistle is essential to control the game. Make coloured sashes for half the number of children so that the teams may be easily identified.

- Play for about 20 minutes each way. It is a good idea to capture the game on video.

- The winning team receives a prize and the rest of the players receive a smaller token. Have a special award ceremony for Most Amazing Goal, Furthest Kick, Happiest Face, and so on.

- Should there be children who aren't able to play or who don't wish to play, they may act as 'team managers' or assist with serving drinks at half time. Uneven numbers of children can also be utilised in this manner.

- No other party games are necessary – children will enjoy ending off this party by watching their video or a sports bloopers video.

Recommended age group: 8–12

FOOTBALL

INVITATIONS

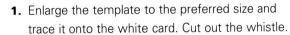

YOU WILL NEED:
Whistle template (page 157)
Stiff white card
Pen or pencil
Scissors
Black felt-tip marker
Red paper
Craft glue
Craft knife
Brightly coloured cord, string or wool
Split ring (similar to that used for key rings)

1. Enlarge the template to the preferred size and trace it onto the white card. Cut out the whistle.
2. Draw in the whistle details with the felt-tip marker. Paste the red paper over the areas as illustrated.
3. Write the invitation details (*see* Suggested wording) on the red paper, trim to size so that it fits on the back of the whistle without protruding. Attach with craft glue.
4. Use a craft knife to cut a slit at the loop end of the whistle before attaching the brightly coloured cord by means of the split ring.

SUGGESTED WORDING

Squad member (guest's name), you've been selected for (birthday child's name) Cup Final.
Stadium: (party address)
Kick off: (date and times of party)
RSVP: referee (or coach) at (phone number) by (date)
Dress: wear sports shoes and suitable clothes for play

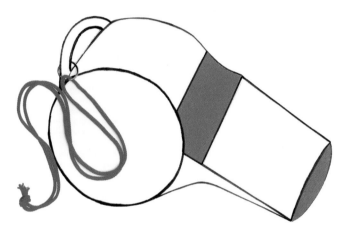

TREAT BAGS

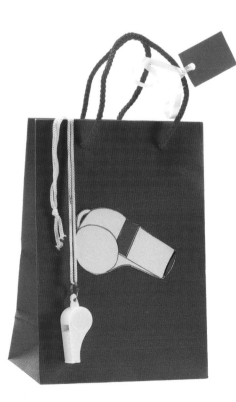

**YOU WILL NEED
(PER BAG):**
Whistle template
(page 157)
Stiff white card
Scissors
Black felt-tip marker
Red paper
Craft glue
Red gift bag
Plastic toy whistle
with cord
Red name card
White curling ribbon

1. Follow steps 1 and 2 of the invitation and glue the whistle onto the gift bag.
2. Attach a toy whistle to the cord handle of the bag.
3. Write the guest's name on the red card and attach it to the cord handle with the curling ribbon.

PARTY FOOD

PENALTY PUNCH

MAKES 5 LITRES
1 litre pineapple juice
1 litre mango juice
1 litre orange juice
2 litres lemonade
Ice cubes

Mix together the fruit juices and add the lemonade and ice cubes just before serving.

OFF-SIDE ORANGES

Oranges
Yellow jelly (powder or cubes)
Red jelly (powder or cubes)
Boiling water

1. Cut the oranges in half and scoop out the flesh, taking care not to pierce the peel. Set the flesh aside – you can serve this as an optional extra.
2. Prepare the jellies according to the package instructions, allow to cool slightly, then pour the jelly into the orange halves. Refrigerate until set.
3. Once the jelly has set, cut each half into two.

CORNER KICK CUPCAKES

Party Cupcakes (page 153)
Icing (page 152) – green
Plastic football player (available at party supply stores)
Round sweet for the ball

1. Prepare the cupcakes according to the recipe and leave to cool completely.
2. Use the star nozzle to decorate the cupcakes with green icing to resemble grass. Position the toy football player and the ball on the cake.

LEAGUE BALL

Party Cupcakes (page 153)
Icing (page 152) – green, black
White gum balls

1. Prepare the cupcakes according to the recipe and leave to cool completely.
2. Use the star nozzle to decorate the cupcakes with green icing to resemble grass. Place a white gum ball on each and pipe on small black spots.

AWARD-WINNING BISCUITS

Easy Biscuits (page 152)
Icing (page 152) – colour of choice
Gold dust
Gold balls
Narrow ribbon, enough to hang
  around a child's neck

1. Prepare the biscuit dough according to the recipe.
2. Cut round shapes from the biscuit dough and use a large drinking straw to make a hole near the edge before baking according to instructions.
3. Allow to cool completely, then ice.
4. Use a toothpick to trace a number 1 in the icing.
5. Dust the biscuit with gold dust and apply the gold balls to the shape of the traced number.
6. Leave the icing to set, then thread the ribbon through the hole, tying a knot at the ends.

OTHER FOOD IDEAS

Header hamburgers: set out buttered rolls, cooked burger patties, and slices of cheese, pineapple, gherkins, tomatoes, and lettuce leaves. The children can assemble their own burgers. Include squeeze bottles of red card (tomato) and yellow card (mustard) sauce.

FOOTBALL STAR CAKE

Basic Cake (page 152) – see note, step 1 below
Icing (page 152) – green, team colours of choice
Plastic doll
Plastic football
Foil-covered chocolate footballs

1. Bake the cake according to the recipe. The doll that I used was 340 mm in length and this dictated the size of the cake – I baked one 330 x 260 mm, then halved the quantity and baked an additional smaller one in a 260 x 180 mm cake tin.
2. Join the two cakes together and cover with green icing to resemble the grass.
3. Place the doll in position and, using the star nozzle, ice clothes in team colours of choice.
4. Add the plastic football and place chocolate footballs around the edge of the cake.

For this party, it is advisable not to have too many guests, as it will be difficult to control and assist the children, unless you have a helper. Preparations should be done well in advance of the date. No games are necessary.

Fabric

SETTING THE SCENE

* Prepare a piece of prewashed, ironed, 100% cotton fabric (300 x 300 mm) for each child. Use pinking scissors or an overlocker to neaten the edges. Copy simple designs that will appeal to the age group and trace onto the fabric using a fabric marking pen.

* Set a place for each child at a low, plastic-covered table with a bowl of water, brush and paper towels. Arrange 125 ml containers of fabric paints (including glitter paints) in easily accessible positions.

* Allow the children to choose a design, then write their names in pencil on the reverse side of the fabric. Give the children the basic instructions – simply wet the brushes and apply the paint, just as they would when colouring a paper drawing – and ensure an adult is available for those who need assistance.

* Prepare an extra square of fabric with a section for each child to portray their creativity and their name, which the birthday child may keep as a memento.

* Award prizes for: Brightest Colours, Most Glitter, Neatest Painting, Most Colours, Least Colours, and so on, thus ensuring that each child receives a prize.

* Provide precut squares of cardboard to which the children may attach their fabric with paper clips if the paint hasn't dried by the time they leave the party.

* Decorate the party area with balloons and streamers and cover the party table with brightly coloured crepe paper sprinkled with confetti. Place bowls of popcorn and sweets on the table so that children may have something to nibble while they work.

Recommended age group: 6-12

Painting

INVITATIONS

YOU WILL NEED (PER INVITATION):
Flower and butterfly template (page 156)
Prewashed and ironed, 100% cotton cloth,
measuring 150 x 200 mm
Fabric marking pen
Fabric paints in
different colours
Pinking scissors
or overlocker
Coloured notepaper
Hair tie or ribbon
Name tags

1. Enlarge the template to the preferred size, or use a design of choice (children's colouring books are a good source of simple designs), and trace it onto the cotton cloth using the fabric marking pen.
2. Paint the design and allow to dry.
3. Trim the edges with a pair of pinking scissors to neaten, or overlock if preferred.
4. Write the details (*see* Suggested wording) on a piece of coloured notepaper, place under the fabric and roll the two up together.
5. Secure with a pretty hair tie or ribbon and attach a name tag.

SUGGESTED WORDING
Create a rainbow of colour at (birthday child's name)'s fabric painting party.
Studio: (address)
Dipping of brushes: (date and times)
RSVP: art teacher at (phone number) by (date)
Dress: old clothes with art shirt or apron

TREAT BAGS

YOU WILL NEED (PER BAG):
Colourful gift bag with cord handles (fairly spacious
to transport the artwork that will be created)
OR
Cardboard box, sprayed with non-toxic craft
spray (punch a hole near the upper
edge on either side of the
box and insert a pipe cleaner
or cord for the handle)
Flower and butterfly
template (page 156)
Coloured notepaper
Craft glue
Glitter glue
Curling ribbon
Paint-fixing
instructions

1. Use the same template as for the invitation and trace it onto the coloured paper, or use white paper and colour with craft paint.
2. Decorate the design as preferred, cut it out and stick it onto the front of the bag.
3. Use glitter glue to write the guest's name on the bag, and tie curling ribbon to the handles.
4. Include instructions for fixing the paint (see below), so that guests' parents will be able to complete a cushion or frame the work.

How to fix the paint
Ensure that the paint is completely dry, then apply a hot iron to the reverse side of the work. Iron the material well for about two minutes.

PARTY FOOD

Tea break

Marshmallow cones (page 153)
Coloured balls or similar to decorate
Pretzel bows
Icing (page 152) – colour of choice
Marie biscuits or Rich Tea™ biscuits
Hundreds and thousands

1. Prepare the marshmallow for the cones and pour the mixture into edible (wafer) cookie cups. top
2. Allow to set then sprinkle with coloured balls or similar decoration.
3. Cut small sections off pretzel bows to resemble the ear of a teacup and, with a small blob of icing, attach to the cookie cup.
4. Ice a Marie or tea biscuit and sprinkle with hundreds and thousands. Place the cookie cup in the centre.

Palette biscuits

Easy Biscuits (page 152)
Palette template (page 156)
Icing (page 152) – white
Astros™ or Skittles™
Liquorice Allsorts™
Candy sticks

1. Prepare the biscuit dough as per the recipe.
2. Enlarge the template to the preferred size, trace it onto cardboard and use it to cut out the biscuits. Bake as per instructions.
3. Allow the biscuits to cool completely, then coat with a layer of white icing.
4. Place about seven differently coloured Astros™ or Skittles™ in position as indicated.
5. Use a slice from a Liquorice Allsorts™ and shape it to resemble the bristles of a brush. Attach it to a candy stick with a small blob of icing.
6. Place in position across the palette.

Colour kaleidoscope

Party Cupcakes (page 153)
Icing (page 152) – white
Brightly coloured lollipops
Small coloured sweets

1. Bake the cupcakes according to the recipe and allow to cool completely.
2. Cover with white icing.
3. Place a lollipop upside down in the centre of the cupcake. Add sweets as illustrated overleaf.

Easy easel

Coconut marshmallows
Toothpicks
Large dome-shaped sugared jelly sweets
Small sweets of choice
Icing (page 152) – colour of choice

1. Insert three toothpicks into the marshmallow so that they form the legs of the easel.
2. Attach a jelly sweet to the base of each toothpick and adjust the legs as necessary so that the easel stands upright.
3. Attach a sweet to the easel with a small dab of icing so that it looks like a painting on an easel.

Other food ideas

Chicken nuggets: with tomato sauce and mustard.
Paint pot jellies: prepare different colours of jelly in small plastic tubs and serve with dainty plastic spoons tied with a delicate curling ribbon.
Rainbow of colour: form a brightly coloured rainbow of toothpicks skewered with sliced cocktail sausages, blocks of cheese, and cocktail onions (green, yellow, red and white).

FABRIC PAINTING CAKE

1 x Basic Cake (page 152) – 330 x 260 mm
Smooth apricot jam, sufficient to coat the cake
Icing sugar for dusting
Sugar paste – white
Flower and butterfly template (page 156)
Powdered food colourings
White alcohol, or water if preferred
Edible glitter
Ribbon (optional)

1. Bake the cake as per the recipe and allow to cool completely. Coat with a thin layer of smooth apricot jam.
2. Dust a board lightly with icing sugar and roll out the sugar paste with a rolling pin, to fit the full size of the cake. Carefully place the rolled sugar paste onto the cake.
3. Enlarge the template to the preferred size, cut it out and place it in position on the sugar paste.
4. Use a toothpick to lightly trace around the outline of the design.
5. Mix a small quantity of powdered colouring with a few drops of alcohol or water until a smooth, runny consistency is obtained.
6. Apply the colour to the design with a small artist's brush.
7. Use a fine brush to outline the petals and the butterfly wings with black colouring.
8. Once the paint has dried, paint over the centre of the flower as well as the spots on the butterfly's wings using edible glitter.
9. Add the birthday child's name as well as their age to a bottom corner of the cake.
10. If desired, wrap a ribbon around the cake to neaten the overall appearance.

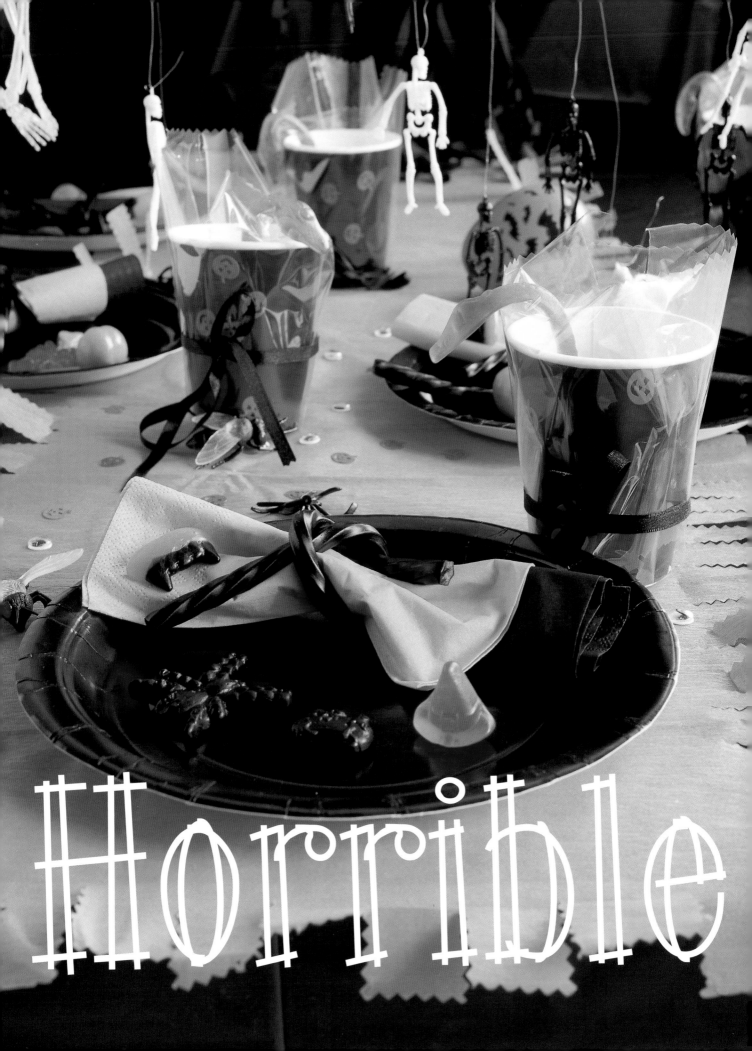

#Horrible

SETTING THE SCENE

* This party is even more fun if it is held in the early evening. It is easy to transform the party venue into a haunted house with the wide range of décor items available. This theme may also be adapted for a Halloween party.

* Mark the path to the party entrance with paper lanterns – half fill a brown paper bag with sand and place a small candle or tealight in the sand. Slightly dampen the bags to prevent them from burning and keep under adult supervision at all times.

* Line the walls and windows with black paper or cloth. Attach plastic toy skeletons to the cloth, or suspend them from the ceiling with fishing line.

* Drape black streamers from the centre of the ceiling to the corners and tie black balloons in bundles and hang them from the ceiling.

* Hang an artificial spider's web in the doorway and attach a few plastic spiders.

* Use fishing line to suspend large plastic spiders and bats from the ceiling.

* If the party is at night, use glow-in-the-dark plastic spiders and skeletons.

* Dim the lighting and provide children with torches to enhance the scary atmosphere.

* Cover the party table with a black cloth and scatter plastic spiders among the food bowls.

* Make ghosts, in the same manner as the invitation, but use large balls or balloons, and a white sheet, and hang from garden trees or from corners of ceilings.

Recommended age group: 9–12

Horrors

INVITATIONS

YOU WILL NEED (PER INVITATION):
Polystyrene ball (the size of a golf ball)
White crepe paper measuring 360 x 360 mm
Elastic band
2 x small googly eyes
Craft glue
Black curling ribbon
Small white stiff card
Black felt-tip marker
Glitter glue

1. Place the ball in the centre of the crepe paper and gather the paper around it. Secure at the 'neck' with an elastic band.
2. Attach the eyes to the 'head' with craft glue.
3. Tie the ribbon around the 'neck'.
4. Write the party details (*see* Suggested wording) on the stiff card, decorate with glitter glue and attach the card to the ribbon on the ghost.

SUGGESTED WORDING
Float over to (birthday child's name)'s party.
Haunted house: (address)
Witching hour: (date and times)
RSVP: the main monster at (phone number) by (date)
Dress: horribly scary

TREAT BAGS

YOU WILL NEED (PER BAG):
Ghost template (page 157)
White paper
Scissors
Craft glue
Small cake box sprayed black with non-toxic craft spray
2 x googly eyes
Black or red felt-tip marker

1. Enlarge the template to the preferred size and trace the ghost onto the white paper. Cut out, then position slightly to the left of the lid of the box and glue it in place.
2. Attach the googly eyes and draw a mouth with a black or red felt-tip marker.
3. Decorate the box as preferred – for example use glitter glue to write 'BOO (guest's name)!' on the right-hand side of the lid.

GAMES AND ACTIVITIES

Help the ghost

YOU WILL NEED:

Boxes of choice, eg a shoe boxes, wrapped in
  different colours or patterns
Range of items to imitate body parts
  (see suggestions below)
Maps for each team
Felt-tip markers
Large poster of a ghost
Surgical glove filled with flour

Hide the boxes throughout the party area. One 'body part' (see suggestions below) is placed in each of these boxes. The boxes must be sealed, with an opening wide enough for a child's hand to pass through.

Suggestions of items to use (how many you choose will depend on the number of children):

Cooked spaghetti = intestines
Peeled litchi = eyeball
Cleaned, boiled chicken bone = leg or arm bone
Uncooked corn kernel = a tooth
Piece of hair cut from an old doll = hair
Bits of steel wool = beard
Dried apricots or pears = ears
Raw chicken liver in a plastic bag = liver
Surgical glove filled with flour = hand
Cottage cheese piped into a coiled shape = brains
Slivered almond = toenail or fingernail
Cornflake = scab
Piece of raw chicken fillet = tongue

Once the children have been welcomed by an adult dressed as a ghost, tell them about the ghosts that live in the party house. Conjure up as many characters as befits the family, but focus on a very sad ghost who has misplaced some of his body parts. Instruct the children that they need to help him find them.

Divide the children into colour-coded teams, give each team a map with clues and dispatch them to find their designated containers. Once located, they must return with their unopened boxes to a designated area.

At this point, break for refreshments.

Back to the mystery game... Each team is given a piece of paper and they take turns, without peeping, to feel the objects inside the boxes to determine what body part they have located. They write their answers on the paper, taking care not to divulge their findings to the other teams. A time limit should be allocated for this section of the game.

Allow the children to wash their hands, then have another break for refreshments.

For the last round of the game, place a large poster of a ghost beside each team. Place a surgical glove filled with flour and sealed with an elastic band alongside the ghost. Teams must, using the 'hand' and a felt-tip marker, draw the body parts that they have identified.

The team members with the most correct definitions receive a prize. Smaller tokens are distributed to the other children.

Spin the web

YOU WILL NEED:

Toy spider
Black wool

Using a big, black, hairy toy spider and black wool, wrap up the spider as you wind the wool into a large ball. (Use more than one ball of wool and attach the two together, if there are many children.)

Instruct the children to stand in a circle. While the birthday child holds onto the end of the wool, the ball is randomly tossed from one child to the other, with each child that catches the ball holding onto a piece of the wool, before passing the ball on, and so creating a web. The last child at the end of the wool gets to keep the spider as a prize.

PARTY FOOD

Toothy treats

Party Cupcakes (page 153)
Icing (page 152) – white, black
Monster teeth sweets
White gum balls
Silver balls

1. Bake the cupcakes as per the recipe and allow to cool completely.
2. Ice the top of the cupcake white and attach the candy teeth for the mouth.
3. Place the gum balls (eyes) in position, apply blobs of icing and attach the silver balls to create the pupils.
4. Ice ribbons of black icing for the hair.

Boo-tiful sweets

Wafer ice-cream cones
Sweets of choice
Marie biscuits or Rich Tea™ biscuits
Icing (page 152) – white
Round lollipops
White paper serviettes
Black ribbon
Felt-tip marker

1. Fill a wafer cone with sweets and place an iced Marie or tea biscuit over the open end. Upend so that the biscuit forms a firm base for the cone.
2. Gently push a round lollipop into the neck of the cone so that only the round bit protrudes.
3. Drape a white serviette over the lollipop and cone, gather up at the 'neck' and tie with a black ribbon. Use a felt-tip marker to draw eyes and a mouth on the 'face'.

Ghoulish hands

These are so easy to prepare – definitely a task that may be allocated to the birthday child!

Plastic food gloves
Large red dome-shaped sugared jelly sweets
Popcorn
Elastic bands

1. Place a large red jellied sweet into each finger of the glove to create the fingernails.
2. Fill the rest of the glove with popcorn and secure the end with an elastic band.

Mr Bones is all heart!

Easy Biscuits (page 152)
Gingerbread man cookie cutter
Icing (page 152) – black, white
White marshmallows
Heart-shaped sweets

1. Prepare the biscuit dough as per the recipe.
2. Use the cookie cutter to cut the dough and bake the biscuits as directed. Allow to cool completely.
3. Cover the entire biscuit with black icing, then use a toothpick to trace the skeleton's bones before filling with white piping.
4. Cut a slice from a marshmallow to use for the head. Pipe on the eyes and mouth.
5. Attach the heart-shaped sweet.

Other food ideas

Crisps with Avocado Dip (page 154)
Popular potions: add a scoop of vanilla ice cream to black or red carbonated cold drinks just before serving.

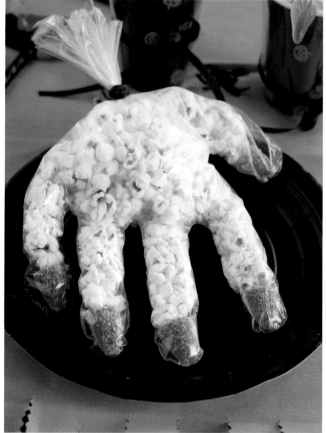

HORRIBLE HORROR CAKE

Unfortunately there will be bits of cake that are not used, but these can be frozen for a small trifle at a later stage!

2 x Basic Cake (page 152) – 250 mm round cake, 330 x 260 mm cake
Icing (page 152) – green, red, black
2 x Marie biscuits or Rich Tea™ biscuits
Gold balls
2 x wafer ice-cream cones
Sugared worm-shaped sweets
Toy monster eyes or decorated gum balls
Liquorice Allsorts Mini™
Liquorice strips
Toy plastic tongue

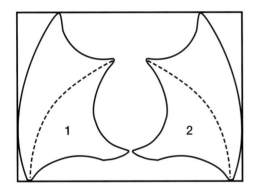 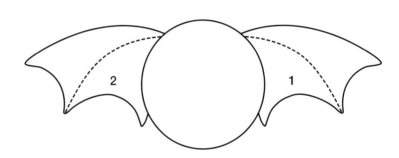

1. Bake the cakes as per the recipe and allow to cool completely.
2. Cut out the wings from the rectangular cake as per the diagram above left.
3. Assemble the cake according to the diagram above right.
4. Cover the face with green icing.
5. Make small incisions to position the Marie or tea biscuit ears and attach the gold balls for the ear studs with icing.
6. Cut the tips off the wafer cones, place a blob of icing in the tip of each cone and insert half a wooden skewer into the cone to allow for easy support when positioned on the head. Decorate these 'horns' with red icing.
7. Position the sugared worms for the hair, and decorate the facial features as follows: toy monster eyes, Liquorice Allsorts Mini™ for the nostrils and liquorice strips for the eyebrows and scar on the cheek.
8. Place the tongue in position.
9. Cover the wings with black icing, and use a star nozzle to outline and to emphasize the veins.

Winter birthday children always envy the pool parties that summer birthday children are able to host. Although the title of this theme may imply blue skies and sandy beaches, this party does not have to be held in summer.

Under

SETTING THE SCENE

✳ Cover a large cardboard box with coloured paper or spray with craft paint and decorate to resemble a treasure chest. Spray a few garden pebbles with gold or silver paint and place around the chest. Place the chest at the entrance for children to deposit their gifts.

✳ Hand each child a bottle of bubbles and allow them to blow bubbles as they wait for the rest of the children to arrive.

✳ Decorate the room with blue and/or green streamers hanging from the ceiling, low enough so that the children feel as if they are walking under the water. Line the walls with blue crepe paper or blue sheets. Use construction paper to make underwater creatures, such as sharks, fish and jellyfish, and suspend them from the ceiling with fishing line. Attach sea creatures to the walls and windows. Octopuses can be made using polystyrene balls, covered with crepe paper, gathered and tied with an elastic band at the neck, and the remaining section under the 'head' cut into eight strips to make the tentacles. Glue googly eyes into position and sprinkle with glitter glue. Suspend a large octopus in the doorway so that children have to pass through its tentacles as they enter.

✳ Cover the floor with shredded blue and green crepe paper.

✳ Cover the party table with blue crepe paper and top with a piece of tulle or organza fabric, bunched in places to create a wavy effect. Scatter crumbled Marie or tea biscuits sparsely over the cloth for sea sand, and place toy sea creatures and shells on the table.

✳ Serve the food from sand moulds or plastic goldfish bowls.

Recommended age group: 6-10

the Sea

INVITATIONS

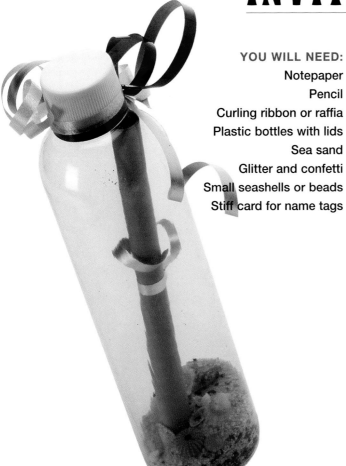

YOU WILL NEED:
Notepaper
Pencil
Curling ribbon or raffia
Plastic bottles with lids
Sea sand
Glitter and confetti
Small seashells or beads
Stiff card for name tags

1. Write the party details (*see* Suggested wording) on the notepaper.
2. Wrap the notepaper firmly around a pencil, to ensure that it is tight enough to fit through the neck of the bottle. Tie firmly with curling ribbon or raffia. Remove the pencil and insert the invitation into the bottle.
3. Add a few teaspoons of sea sand to the bottle together with some glitter, confetti and a few small seashells or beads.
4. Put the lid on the bottle and tie curling ribbon or raffia around the neck.
5. Write the guest's name on the stiff card and attach to the ribbon.

SUGGESTED WORDING
Celebrate (birthday child's name) birthday under the sea.
Coral reef: (address)
Take the plunge on: (date)
High tide: (party starts)
Low tide: (party ends)
RSVP: Neptune at (phone number) by (date)

TREAT BAGS

YOU WILL NEED (PER BOX):
Fish template (page 157)
Small cake box
Craft paint in various bright colours
Glitter
Googly eye
Craft glue

Two lengths of pipe cleaner, about 90 mm and 60 mm respectively
Aquarium stones
Glitter glue

1. Enlarge the template to the preferred size. Trace it onto the lid of the cake box and colour brightly using craft paints and glitter.
2. Attach a googly eye to the fish.
3. Use craft glue to affix the two lengths of pipe cleaner to the box, to form sea weed, and add the aquarium stones around the base.
4. Lightly brush the stones with glitter glue.
5. Write the guest's name on the lid.

GAMES AND ACTIVITIES

Deep-sea fishing

YOU WILL NEED:
Wooden dowel rods with hooks
Toy fish
Small hooks
Kiddies' paddling pool

It is not necessary to have a dowel for each child as they can take turns.

Attach the small hooks to the toy fish or other sea creatures and submerge them in a kiddies' paddling pool filled with water. Attach numbers to the fish so that the children may choose a correspondingly numbered gift from a basket. They also get to keep the fish they have nabbed.

Once the children have managed to catch a fish they are eliminated, thus ensuring each child is successful. Remember to make one or two extra fish so that the last child also has a fair choice.

Pin the pearl in the oyster

YOU WILL NEED:
Large poster paper
Felt-tip marker
Rounds made from stiff board for the pearls
Double-sided tape
Blindfold

Draw a large oyster on the sheet of poster paper. Write each child's name on a pearl and attach a piece of double-sided tape to the back.

The children take turns to be blindfolded, spun about three times and to place their pearl in the oyster.

The pearl nearest the centre wins a prize, the rest of the children receive tokens.

Deep-sea snorkelling

YOU WILL NEED (PER TEAM):
Diving goggles
Pair of flippers
Pair of men's pyjamas

Divide the children into two or more teams and have them stand in line, one behind the other.

The front child in each team puts on the pyjamas, flippers and goggles and, on starter's orders, runs to a designated point and back to his team, where he or she must undress and hand the apparel to the second child, before taking up position at the back of the row.

The game continues in the same manner until the first child reaches the front of the row again. The winning team receives a prize, the rest receive tokens.

Electric eel leap

YOU WILL NEED:
Skipping rope

Spread the rope along the ground with a volunteer holding onto each end. The rope is moved, on the ground, in a swaying motion.

The children must take turns jumping over the eel without touching the rope. With each successive round, the swaying becomes more rapid, with those who are stung by the eel being eliminated.

PARTY FOOD

Great White tooth

Shark tooth template (page 157)
Easy Biscuits (page 152)
White icing or white baking chocolate
Length of cord

1. Enlarge the template to the preferred size and cut out.
2. Prepare the biscuit dough according to the recipe and use the template to cut out the biscuits.
3. Make a hole near the top with a drinking straw.
4. Bake as directed and allow to cool completely.
5. Coat with icing or melted chocolate.
6. Allow the icing to set completely before threading a cord through the hole so that the children may wear the tooth as a necklace.

Sparkling starfish

Party Cupcakes (page 153)
Icing (page 152) – blue, orange
Silver balls

1. Bake the cupcakes according to the recipe and allow to cool completely.
2. Cover the tops of the cupcakes with blue icing.
3. Use a toothpick to mark five lines from the centre to the edges.
4. Using the star nozzle and orange icing, pipe a starfish shape onto the cake.
5. Decorate with silver balls.

Other food ideas

Fish bowl: blue jelly with plastic sea creatures 'swimming' inside.
Riding the surf: skewer a dolphin-shaped sweet on a toothpick and insert in a Meringue (page 153).

Floating icebergs

Blue or green carbonated drinks
Vanilla ice cream
Paper parasols
Frilly drinking straws (page 154)

1. Pour the cold drinks into plastic parfait glasses to about two-thirds full.
2. Add a scoop of vanilla ice cream to each glass.
3. Insert a paper parasol and serve with a frilly straw.

School of fish

Easy Biscuits (page 152)
Fish-shaped cookie cutter
Icing (page 152) – colours of choice
Silver balls

1. Prepare the biscuit dough as per the recipe. Use the fish-shaped cookie cutter to cut out the biscuits.
2. Bake as directed and allow to cool completely.
3. Use bright-coloured icing to decorate, placing a silver ball in position for the eye.

Odyssey of an octopus

Marie biscuits or Rich Tea™ biscuits
Icing (page 152) – colour of choice
Sour worm-shaped sweets
Round apricot sweets
Silver balls

1. Coat the biscuit with icing. Position the worm sweets from the centre outwards to resemble the tentacles.
2. Place the round sweet in the centre and decorate the face as shown.

FANCY FISH CAKE

This cake should be baked at least one to two days before icing to ensure that it is firm when cutting to assemble.

1 x Basic Cake (page 152) – baked in two x 220 mm round cake tins
Icing (page 152) – blue, yellow
2 x large googly eyes
1 x round red sugared gum sweet
Flat yellow sweets
Large silver balls
Small round yellow sweets
Wooden skewers

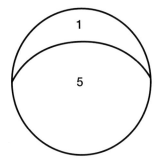 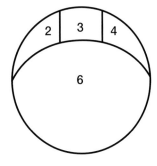

1. As advised, one or two days before icing, bake the cakes as per the recipe.
2. Cut out sections from each cake as per the template above.
3. Sandwich sections 5 and 6 together with a layer of icing.
4. Use a toothpick to outline the head and the stripes on both sides of the cake.
5. Coat the cut edge with icing and place the cake on a serving platter – in an upright position – with the cut edge resting on the platter.
6. Ice the body of the fish as illustrated and position the eyes and the red gum sweet for the mouth.
7. Decorate the stripes with the flat yellow sweets and silver balls.
8. Coat the edges of section 1, which is the tail fin, and attach it to the body of the fish using at least two wooden skewers to secure, allowing it to 'rest' on the platter.
9. Coat the tail with icing and attach the small yellow sweets.
10. Section 2 is placed in position for the top fin, again securing with a skewer and covering with icing.
11. Section 4 is cut in half horizontally to form the two side fins. Secure with skewers if necessary and coat with icing.
12. Section 3 is discarded.

The dinosaur remains a favourite theme for the younger child. It is an easy party to arrange as most children have dinosaur toys that can be used to create a prehistoric wonderland.

SETTING THE SCENE

✳ Enlarge the footprint template (page 156) to the preferred size and trace it onto stiff green poster board. Lay a path of footprints from the gate to the entrance of the party.

✳ Place all available pot plants at the entrance and suspend garden creepers and/or green streamers in the doorway to create a prehistoric jungle.

✳ Drape green streamers from the centre of the ceiling to the corners and suspend cardboard pterodactyls from the ceiling using fishing line, so that they swoop over the table.

✳ Tie green balloons in bundles and place in strategic positions.

✳ If you have them, inflatable dinosaurs will add to the effect.

✳ Cover the party table with a green table cloth and place empty upturned plastic bowls under the cloth to create a mountainous effect.

✳ Toy dinosaurs may be displayed on the table and in any other room that may be used, such as the bathroom.

Recommended age group: 3-6

Dinosaurs

INVITATIONS

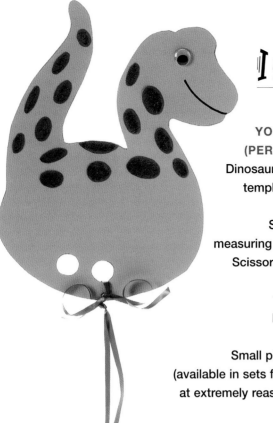

**YOU WILL NEED
(PER INVITATION):**
Dinosaur finger puppet
template (page 155)
Pen or pencil
Stiff green card
measuring 250 x 200 mm
Scissors or craft knife
Craft glue
1 x googly eye
Felt-tip marker
Ribbon
Small plastic dinosaur
(available in sets from toy stores
at extremely reasonable prices)

1. Enlarge the template to the preferred size and trace it onto the stiff green card. Cut out along the outline, and cut out the two finger holes.
2. Glue a googly eye onto the side of the head and draw in the mouth with a felt-tip marker.
3. Decorate the body as preferred.
4. Write the party details (*see* Suggested wording) on the back of the card.
5. Tie a ribbon through one of the finger holes and attach a toy dinosaur.

SUGGESTED WORDING
Join (birthday child's name) on a dinosaur discovery!
Swamp location: (address)
Exploration starts: (date and time of start of party)
Extinction: (party ends)
RSVP: expedition leader at (phone number) by (date)

TREAT BAGS

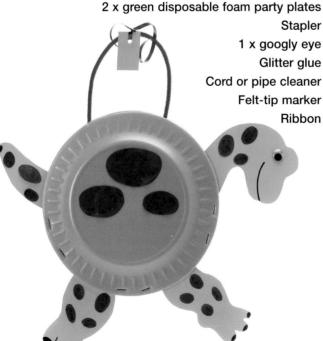

YOU WILL NEED (PER BAG):
Dinosaur template (page 156)
Stiff green card
Scissors or craft knife
Craft glue
2 x green disposable foam party plates
Stapler
1 x googly eye
Glitter glue
Cord or pipe cleaner
Felt-tip marker
Ribbon

1. Enlarge the template to the preferred size and trace it onto the stiff green card.
2. Cut out the body parts and glue them to the 'inside' of one of the paper plates, close to the edge, so that the head and tail stick out on either side of the upper half of the plate, while the legs protrude at the bottom.
3. Place the second paper plate over this, 'bottom' side up, and, leaving an opening at the top, staple the two plates together.
4. Attach a googly eye to the head of the dinosaur and decorate the plate (body) with glitter circles as illustrated.
5. Attach a cord or pipe cleaner on either side of the opening.
6. Write the guest's name on a green card with glitter glue or a felt-tip marker and attach it to the bag's cord with a ribbon.

GAMES AND ACTIVITIES

Dinosaur footprints

YOU WILL NEED:
Dinosaur footprints made from template, page 156
  (make extra or recycle those from the pathway)
Music

Make the footprints as described on page 115. Ensure that there are sufficient footprints for the number of children, less one.

Lay a track of footprints that children skip around in time to music. When the music stops, the children must hop onto a footprint and the child who is unable to secure one is eliminated.

Remove one print before starting the music once more. The game continues in this manner until there is a winner, who receives a prize. The rest of the children receive smaller tokens.

Pass the hatching egg

YOU WILL NEED:
Dinosaur toy
Wrapping paper
Smaller tokens for each layer of paper
Music

Wrap a dinosaur toy in numerous layers of paper – with a small token or a sticker (not affixed) attached to each layer so that most children receive a small token – and have the children sit in a circle.

As music plays, the children must pass the egg from one to another until the music stops. The child holding the egg when the music stops must unwrap a layer of paper. They get to keep the small token attached.

The child who unwraps the last layer of paper wins the prize (the dinosaur toy).

Return the T-Rex's eggs

YOU WILL NEED:
2 x bags of round sweets, sufficient for the
  number of children
2 x tablespoons
Two receptacles for 'nests'
Red cloth or crepe paper for lava
Dinosaur feet (optional) – template, page 156

Divide the children into two teams. Provide each team with a bag of 'eggs' (round sweets), ensuring that there are sufficient eggs in each bag for the number of children, as well as a spoon.

Place a 'nest' for each team at one end of the playing area, and position a winding river of molten lava (red crepe paper or other red cloth) between the nest and the team.

On starter's orders, the first child in each team must place an 'egg' on the spoon and, without dropping it, must jump over the river, place the egg in the nest, return to the team, again jumping over the lava, and pass the spoon to the next child, who must follow the same procedure.

The game continues in this manner until all the eggs have been placed in the nest. If an egg is dropped, the child must return to the team and start once more. The winning team receives a prize, the rest receive a token.

To make the task more challenging, dinosaur feet may be fashioned using the template provided and attaching an elastic cord so that the children are able to wear them.

Each team is provided with a set of feet that is passed from child to child at the spoon exchange.

PARTY FOOD

Erupting volcanoes

Wafer ice-cream cones
Dinosaur-shaped sweets
Marie biscuits or Rich Tea™ biscuits
Icing (page 152) – chocolate, red
Sparklers

1. Fill a wafer cone with a few dinosaur sweets.
2. Place a Marie or tea biscuit over the top and secure with icing. Upend the cone so that the biscuit forms the base. Cut the tip off the cone.
3. Coat the outside of the cone with chocolate icing, then use the red icing to decorate the open end of the cone and streak it down (erupting lava).
4. Place a sparkler in each volcano.
5. The sparklers must be lit only under strict adult supervision (have a helper). Care must be taken that the children don't touch the hot rods after the sparklers have burned down.
6. Remove the spent rods immediately and dispose of safely.

A fossil find

Wafer biscuits or Easy Biscuits (page 152)
Chocolate icing (page 152)
Banana-shaped sweets
Bone-shaped sweets
Liquorice Allsorts™

1. Coat the biscuits with chocolate icing.
2. Attach the banana-shaped sweets for the ribs, and place two bone-shaped sweets in position.
3. For the skull, separate the layers of a Liquorice Allsorts™ sweet and use a pair of kitchen scissors to shape it. Use a toothpick or skewer to pierce the skull to make an eye socket before attaching the skull to the biscuit.

Dinosaur nest

Party Cupcakes (page 153)
Icing (page 152) – green, brown
Desiccated coconut, coloured green
Silver balls
Plastic dinosaurs

1. Bake the cupcakes according to the recipe and leave to cool. Top with a layer of green icing.
2. Sprinkle the coconut lightly over the cupcakes.
3. Place the toy dinosaur on the cake, pushing in gently to secure.
4. Pipe a small nest with brown icing and attach three silver balls for the eggs.

Prehistoric punch

MAKES ABOUT 3.5 LITRES
750 ml orange juice
500 ml mango juice
1 x 450 g tin pineapple pieces, including juice
2 litres ginger ale
Dinosaur ice cubes – place dinosaur toys in ice cube trays, add water and freeze

1. Mix the orange juice, mango juice and pineapple together in a large punch bowl.
2. Before serving, add the ginger ale and ice cubes.

Other food ideas

Volcanic rocks with lava sauce: skewer Mini Meatballs (page 154) on toothpicks and serve with tomato sauce.
Stegosaurus spa: chop up green jelly, add Chocolate Oat Drops (page 153), and serve in plastic tubs.

DINO CAKE

It is time-consuming to use the star nozzle for this cake, but the result is well worth it as it adds the perfect texture. Nevertheless, the dinosaur will be equally as handsome with a smooth coating of icing. It is advisable to ice the body and the tail sections before assembly as it is rather awkward to reach the inner tail if using the star nozzle.

2 x Basic Cake (page 152) – two x 250 mm round cakes
Icing (page 152) – green, yellow
Wooden skewers
1 x 100 g packet green wafer biscuits
1 x red jelly sweet
2 x Liquorice Allsorts Mini™
2 x large googly eyes
20 x banana-shaped sweets

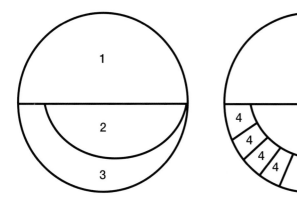

1. Bake the cakes according to the recipe and leave to cool completely.
2. Cut the cakes as per the cake layout above and sandwich sections 1 together with a layer of icing.
3. Coat the cut section with icing as well and place cut edge down on the cake board to create the body. Ice as illustrated. If using the star nozzle, it is advisable to coat the cake with a thin layer of icing first in order to achieve the contour.
4. Sandwich sections 2 together and place in position for the head, with the tapered section forming the snout. Ice as illustrated.
5. Section 3 is for the tail. Ice as illustrated.
6. The smaller sections 4 are used for the legs, with the remaining cake being utilized as extra padding where the head joins the body and up the front curvature of the back. Ice as illustrated.
7. Attach the tail and the feet to the body using wooden skewers where necessary.
8. Decorate the spine with wafer biscuits as shown.
9. Add the facial features – red jelly sweet for the mouth, Liquorice Allsorts™ for the nostrils, and two googly eyes.
10. Place the banana-shaped sweets in position on the feet and the tail for the claws and spikes.
11. If preferred, surround the dinosaur with miniature palm or fern pot plants.

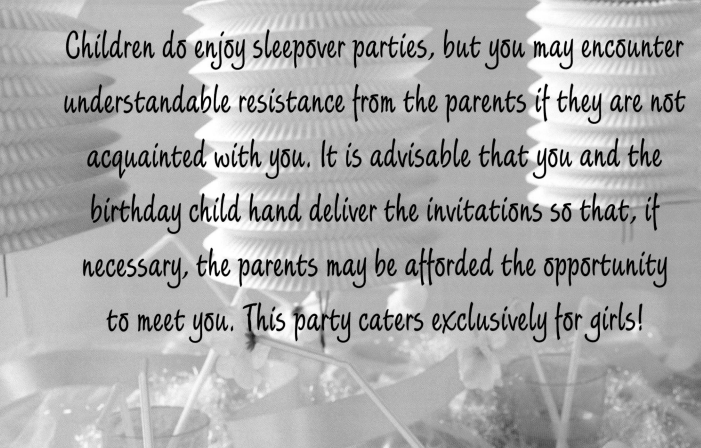

Children do enjoy sleepover parties, but you may encounter understandable resistance from the parents if they are not acquainted with you. It is advisable that you and the birthday child hand deliver the invitations so that, if necessary, the parents may be afforded the opportunity to meet you. This party caters exclusively for girls!

SETTING THE SCENE

This setting can be readily adapted to your child's preferences. For a starry, glitzy evening, do the following:

* Drape black streamers from the centre of the ceiling to the corners, with bundles of black and silver balloons.

* Suspend glow-in-the-dark moons and stars from the ceiling with fishing line.

* Hang mirrors on the walls, if possible.

* Decorate the walls with fashion posters.

* Cover the party table with black crepe paper. Place a large mirror on top of the paper and sprinkle with silver star confetti.

For a more 'girly' evening, try this:

* Drape the walls with yellow sheets or crepe paper.

* Hang Chinese paper lanterns above the party table.

* Cover the party table with pink cloth or crepe paper, with ruched yellow tulle over the top.

* Scatter silk flowers and shredded glitter foil over the table.

Recommended age group: 8–12

Sleepover

INVITATIONS

YOU WILL NEED (PER INVITATION):
Calico or fabric of choice measuring 400 x 120 mm
Needle and thread
Notepaper
Black or yellow ribbon
Stiff card
Glitter glue

1. Fold the material in half and sew the side seams together, leaving the top end open.
2. Neaten the top edge by turning under a hem of about 20 mm.
3. Write the invitation details (*see* Suggested wording) on the notepaper, and cut it to size to fit into the 'sleeping bag'.
4. Insert the paper and roll up the sleeping bag.
5. Secure with the ribbon. Write the guest's name on the card and decorate with glitter glue. Slip the card under the ribbon.

SUGGESTED WORDING
Unroll your sleeping bag and prepare to be pampered at (birthday child's name)'s sleepover party!
Beauty salon: (address)
Makeover appointment: (date and time)
Rooms need to be vacated: (date and time)*
RSVP: beauty therapist @ (phone number) by (date)
Bring pyjamas, sleeping bag, pillow and personal toiletries (toothbrush, facecloth).

* Note to Birthday Mom – it is important to stipulate a 'collection' time as it is a long party and you will need a rest afterwards!

TREAT BAGS

YOU WILL NEED:
Empty tissue boxes or any other suitable carton
Stiff card or pretty ribbon for the handle
Non-toxic black or yellow craft spray
Glow-in-the-dark stars
Name tags decorated with glitter glue
Curling ribbon

1. Cut a length of stiff card and attach it to the tissue box to form a handle.
2. Spray both with craft spray.
3. Decorate the box with the stars and attach the name card with curling ribbon.

GAMES AND ACTIVITIES

Due to the nature of this party, games are not included except for one, which serves as an icebreaker.

Sparkly toes

YOU WILL NEED:
2 x bottles of different-coloured nail varnish
Small paper towels
Music

Instruct the girls to sit in a circle with their bare feet resting on a paper towel and their toes pointing to the centre of the circle. Provide two containers of nail polish at opposite sides of the circle.

When the music starts, both containers must be passed from one girl to another. When the music stops, the children holding the nail polish must each paint one toenail.

Ensure that the lids are secure before restarting the music for the next round! The game continues in this fashion until one child has all ten toenails painted.

Beauty workshop

Ensure that there are plenty of towels to protect the children's clothes, and recruit a helper to assist!

YOU WILL NEED:
Five work stations with:
Face make-up, lip gloss, bright eye shadows
False finger nails and manicure necessities with
    funky shades of nail polish and nail stickers
Temporary tattoos and body paints and glitters
Accessories for hair, together with hair brushes,
    hair gels, hair glitters and coloured hair sprays
Dress up clothes (sufficient for all the girls),
    including plenty of accessories

Divide the girls into pairs and together they will move through the various workstations, according to a preset time limit. The work stations are numbered to ensure consecutive order – each pair draw a card from a hat to determine their starting point.

At the work stations, the pair assist each other with make-up, hair, manicures, and so on. Allow sufficient time so that they don't have to rush through the 'pampering'. When the time is up, the girls will have a fashion parade where they can 'strut their stuff' on the catwalk in time to their favourite music.

Prizes may be awarded in categories that will ensure that each child receives one, for example Most Glitter in Hair, Brightest Lipstick, Shortest Hair, etc.

If possible, record the fashion parade on camera so that they can watch it from their sleeping bags.

Extras

- Provide make-up remover before bedtime.
- Hire videos that will appeal to the children.
- Set out an autograph book for children to sign for the birthday child to keep as a memento.
- Provide a torch for them to use should they require it during the night.

PARTY FOOD

Twinkle star nail varnish

Wafer ice-cream cones
Small sweets of choice
Marie biscuits or Rich Tea™ biscuits
Icing (page 152) – colour of choice
Liquorice Allsorts™ squares
Small star-shaped sweets
Lollipops
Large dome-shaped sugared jelly sweets
Silver balls

1. Place some small sweets in the ice-cream cones.
2. Coat a Marie or tea biscuit with icing and seal the open end of the cone.
3. Upend the cone and snip off the tapered end about halfway up the cone.
4. Coat the cone with icing and add a layer of the square Liquorice Allsorts™ and a star-shaped sweet to create the 'label'.
5. Coat the edge of the tapered opening with icing, then seal with the lollipop. Add an upturned sugared domed sweet to the stick.
6. Decorate the base of the cone with silver balls.

Makeover Molly

Party Cupcakes (page 153)
Icing (page 152) – flesh-coloured, yellow
Red lip-shaped sweets
Astros™ or Skittles™
Liquorice strips
Silver balls

1. Bake the cupcakes according to the recipe and allow to cool completely.
2. Coat the top of the cupcakes with flesh-coloured icing. Use the sweets to add the facial features as illustrated.
3. Ice the hair with yellow icing and add the silver balls to make the little shiny hair clips.

Sleepy time slippers

Slipper template (page 157)
Wafer biscuits
Icing (page 152) – colour of choice
Hundreds and thousands
Sweets of choice

1. Use the template to trace the slipper shape onto a firm piece of cardboard. Cut out.
2. Place the slipper template on a wafer biscuit and cut out the shape with a sharp knife.
3. Ice the front end of the slipper as illustrated, using the star nozzle to create a fluffy appearance.
4. Sprinkle with hundreds and thousands and add a sweet of choice.

Babes in blankets

Meringues (page 153)
Jelly Babies™
Fresh cream

1. Prepare the meringue mixture as per the recipe and pipe rounds, or drop dessertspoonfuls onto a baking tray. Flatten slightly with the back of a spoon and bake according to instructions.
2. Before serving, place a Jelly Baby™ on top of the meringue and, leaving the head exposed, cover the Jelly Baby™ with a blanket of whipped cream.

Other food ideas

Creamy chocolate milkshakes
Chicken drumsticks: serve with tomato sauce and chutney.
Colourful kebabs: alternate mushrooms, cherry tomatoes and cucumber slices on wooden skewers and serve with a dip of choice.

SWEET DREAMS CAKE

1 x Basic Cake (page 152) – 330 x 260 mm
Icing (page 152) – yellow, white
Sugar paste, plain white and coloured pink
4 x small dolls of choice
Striped marshmallow twists or boudoir biscuits
Sweets of choice
2 x Oreo® biscuits
2 x pink marshmallows for the lamp bases
2 x candy sticks
2 x edible (wafer) cookie cups
Desiccated coconut, coloured lemon yellow

1. Bake the cake according to the recipe and allow to cool completely.
2. Coat the entire cake with yellow icing.
3. Mould pillows out of white sugar paste, then place the dolls on the bed.
4. Cover the bed with a blanket of pink sugar paste, allowing it to drape over the edges of the bed.
5. Cut the marshmallow twists or boudoir biscuits in half to make the headboard, positioning them along the top edge of the bed and pressing slightly into the icing to adhere.
6. Decorate the bed cover with sweets of choice, then pipe a thin line of white icing along the upper edge, using the star nozzle, to enhance the appearance.
7. To make the bedside lamps, cover an Oreo® biscuit with pink sugar paste and position a pink marshmallow on top with a dot of icing.
8. Push a candy stick into the marshmallow.
9. Place a blob of icing inside the base of a wafer cookie cup. Turn it upside down and position on the candy stick.
10. Create a fluffy carpet with lemon-coloured desiccated coconut.

For breakfast the following morning

Lay out a self-service spread consisting of:

Muffins
Selection of jams
Grated cheese
Fruit juice
A selection of seasonal fruits
Flavoured yoghurts

This party may be held in the early evening
and the duration extended to about 4 hours.

Karaoke

SETTING THE SCENE

* Consult your local directory for karaoke hire, but remember to book early to avoid disappointment. An alternative is to transcribe popular lyrics onto sheets of paper (these may be sourced from the Internet if necessary), plug a microphone into a hi-fi system and play the relevant music in the background while the star performs. Attach the lyric sheets to a piece of cardboard, to allow for easier handling and better durability.

* Cover the table with silver cloth and a red crepe paper overlay. Alternatively, attach posters of pop stars to the top of the party table and cover with a sheet of clear plastic.

* Sprinkle music note confetti over the table.

* Display pop star posters on the walls.

* Tie bundles of silver and black balloons together and attach to strategic spots.

* Make silver stars and CDs from cardboard and suspend from the ceiling with fishing line or ribbons.

* Set aside an area for the performances – drape curtains or large cloths to form a stage area.

* Arrange chairs for the judges, as well as chairs for the audience.

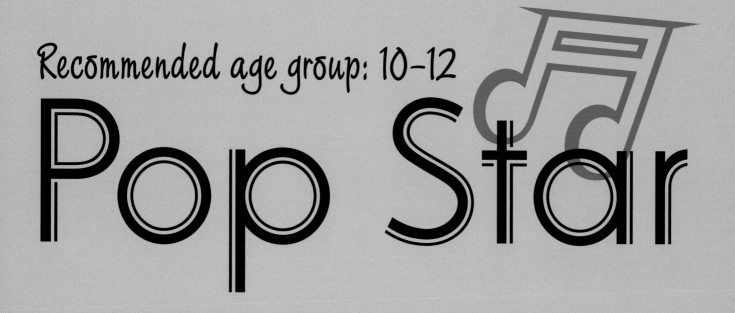

Recommended age group: 10–12

Pop Star

INVITATIONS

YOU WILL NEED (PER INVITATION):
Stiff silver board measuring 130 x 130 mm
Scissors
Felt-tip marker
Plastic CD case

1. Cut the silver board to resemble a CD and write the party details (*see* Suggested wording) on the back.
2. Decorate the front of the CD as desired, then insert it into the case.

SUGGESTED WORDING

(Birthday child's name) is having a karaoke blast on (date) from (start time to end time).
Recording studio: (address)
RSVP: production manager at (phone number) by (date)
Dress: as your favourite pop star

TREAT BAGS

YOU WILL NEED:
Musical note template (page 156)
Stiff black paper
Scissors
Craft glue
Silver gift bags
Black felt-tip marker
Sequins

1. Enlarge the template to the preferred size and trace it onto the black paper. Cut it out and paste onto the front of the gift bag.
2. Write the guest's name on the back of the bag using the felt-tip marker.
3. Use craft glue to attach the sequins.

ACTIVITIES

Karaoke is the sole activity at this party – no other games or activities will be necessary.

When the children arrive, give each one a copy of the list of songs available to select their preference. Once they have made their selection, compile a list of the children's names and their chosen song so that this may be announced by the MC (an adult volunteer).

Children may prefer to perform in groups of two or three; those who do not wish to participate may act as the judges.

Provide two dressing areas where the children will be able to apply make-up, hair accessories, tattoos, and so on. Set aside time for this as well as allowing them time to practise their routine.

When the time comes to start the performances, have the MC call up each child in turn, starting with the birthday child.

While the children await their turn to perform, they fill in as the audience.

After each performance, the judges take turns to pull a comment from a hat (these are obviously prepared in advance), for example 'you certainly have what it takes to become a pop star', 'you sing that better than …' (name of pop star), 'judging from the applause, the audience are going to make you a star', and so on.

At the end of all the performances, there should be a prize for each child that takes the form of 'Best Singer', 'Best Dance Routine', 'Best Hair Style', and so forth. The judges should also receive a prize for their contribution, for example 'Most Complimentary', 'Most Encouraging', 'Most Supportive', etc.

Once the supervised entertainment is over and the food has been served, children will be happy to dance and sing for the rest of the party.

PARTY FOOD

Tambourine biscuits

Marie biscuits or Rich Tea™ biscuits
Icing (page 152) – colour of choice
Small foil-covered chocolate coins
Star-shaped sweets

1. Coat one Marie or tea biscuit with icing on one side only.
2. Position about five chocolate coins on the icing so that half of the coin protrudes over the edge of the biscuit.
3. Coat one side of another biscuit with icing and place this on top of the first, pressing down gently so that it adheres to the coins.
4. Coat the outside of the tambourine with icing and decorate with the star-shaped sweets.

Magic microphones

Silver tinsel pipe cleaners
Wafer ice-cream cones
Sweetie Pies® or Tunnock's Tea Cakes™
Icing (page 152) – colour of choice
Silver vermicelli and silver balls

1. Wind the pipe cleaner around the cone, leaving some extending beyond the tip for the cord.
2. Coat the bottom of the Sweetie Pie® or tea cake with icing and attach to the cup of the cone to form the microphone section. Coat the rest of the Sweetie Pie® or tea cake with icing and cover with vermicelli and silver balls.
3. To make the cones easy to handle, cut the bottom off an egg box and place over a deep bowl, balancing the cones in the holes.

Guitar biscuits

Easy Biscuits (page 152)
Guitar template (page 156)
Chocolate icing (page 152) or melted chocolate
Uncooked spaghetti pieces, cut to size
Gold balls

1. Prepare the biscuit dough as per the recipe.
2. Enlarge the template and trace it onto cardboard. Cut out the guitar and use it to cut the dough.
3. Make a hole in the centre of the widest section, as shown (I used the back of a small icing nozzle).
4. Bake as directed and allow to cool completely.
5. Coat with icing or melted chocolate, then use a toothpick to clear the open section.
6. Position three pieces of spaghetti for the guitar strings and finish off by attaching the gold balls.

Judge's juice

Tall-stemmed, plastic 'champagne-type' glasses
Saucer of pineapple juice
Saucer containing equal quantities of pink jelly powder and sugar mixed together
Cherries
Chunks of pineapple (tinned or fresh)
Variety of pure fruit juices, chilled
Paper parasols

1. Rim the glasses by first dipping them into the pineapple juice and then into the jelly powder and sugar mixture. Leave to set.
2. Assemble the cherries and pineapple chunks onto toothpicks.
3. Pour the chilled fruit juice into the glass, wedge the pineapple onto the rim and add the parasol.

DRUM CAKE

1½ x Basic Cake (page 152) – baked in three x 220 mm round cake tins
Icing (page 152) – white
Flat round sweets
Large dome-shaped sweets
Candy sticks, cut to size
Star-shaped sweets
2 x lengths of liquorice twists
2 x large red gum balls or glacé cherries

1. Bake the cakes as per the recipe and allow to cool completely.
2. Assemble the three cakes on top of each other, with icing between each layer.
3. Coat the top and sides of the cake with smooth white icing.
4. Position the flat and dome-shaped sweets around the top and bottom outside edges of the drum.
5. Position the candy sticks as illustrated, with the star-shaped sweets in between. If preferred, fill the open spaces with other sweets of choice.
6. Attach the gum balls or cherries with icing to one end of the liquorice twists and position on the top of the cake to resemble drum sticks.

This party may be more suitable for boys, although younger girls may enjoy it just as much. Tools and other plastic toys are readily available and reasonably priced, which makes shopping for party favours and prizes quite a pleasure.

Men at

SETTING THE SCENE

* Tie striped black-and-yellow construction tape (or use yellow crepe paper cut into strips) from the front gate to cordon off a pathway leading to the party room. Cut out a triangular board with a sign that says 'Danger: Party in Progress' and place it at the entrance.

* Place orange construction cones along the path leading to the entrance. (These are available in various sizes at discount plastic stores.)

* Use bundles of black and yellow balloons in the party room and drape black and yellow streamers from the centre of the ceiling to the corners of the room.

* Cut out tools (hammers, spanners, and so on) from construction paper and suspend them from the ceiling with fishing line or display them on the party table.

* Cover the table with grey or yellow cloth and black crepe paper or corrugated board. Place rolled up towels or upturned plastic bowls underneath to create an uneven 'building terrain'. Place toy tools or construction vehicles on the table as decoration.

* Use toy construction hats and plastic dump trucks for serving food, and use toy spades as serving spoons.

Recommended age group: 3–8

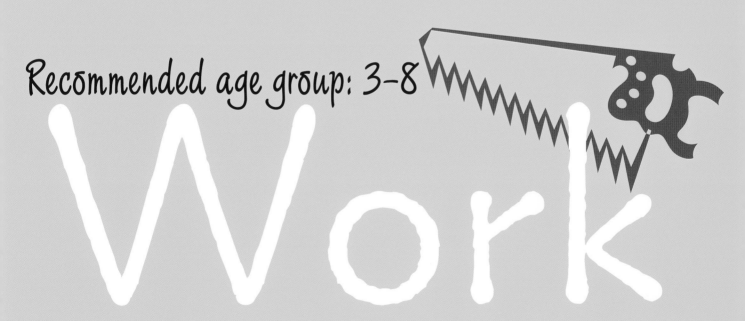

Work

INVITATIONS

YOU WILL NEED (PER INVITATION):
House template (page 155)
Pen or pencil
2 x sheets of construction paper, one red and one yellow, measuring 180 x 180 mm
Craft knife
Craft glue
Clear acetate measuring 140 x 140 mm
Felt-tip marker
Glitter glue

1. Enlarge the template to the preferred size and trace the outline on the two pieces of construction paper.
2. On the yellow paper, draw the windows with a pencil and use a craft knife to cut out the panes. Lay the yellow sheet over the red sheet of paper, and trace the windows onto the red sheet.
3. Glue the piece of clear acetate to the back of the yellow paper so that it covers all the windows.
4. On the red sheet of construction paper, write in the party details (*see* Suggested wording) so that they will show through the window panes.
5. Glue the two sheets together.
6. Use glitter glue along the bottom edge of the building to resemble builder's sand.

SUGGESTED WORDING
Report for duty at (child's name)'s construction party.
Building site: (address)
Laying of foundations: (date)
Shift: (time)
RSVP: site foreman at (phone number) by (date)
Dress: overalls or work clothes

TREAT BAGS

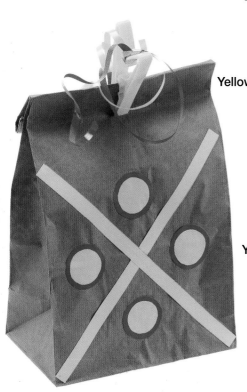

YOU WILL NEED:
Brown paper bags
Yellow craft paper and/or yellow tape
Red craft paper
Scissors
Craft glue
Red and black felt-tip markers
Yellow plastic clothes pegs
Yellow curling ribbon
Red curling ribbon

1. Cut two strips of yellow paper, about 20 cm x 10 mm, and glue onto the front of the bag in the shape of an X. (Or use yellow tape if preferred.)
2. Make the signs by drawing four circles on the red paper, about 30 mm diameter, and smaller circles of about 25 mm in diameter on the yellow paper.
3. Cut out and glue the yellow circles to the centre of the red circles. Use the felt-tip markers on the yellow circles to create signs such as 'No Entry' and 'Caution!', and glue onto the bags.
4. Write the guest's name on the back of the bag with the red or black marker.
5. Close by folding down the top of the packet and secure with a clothes peg. Attach yellow and red curling ribbon to the peg.

GAMES AND ACTIVITIES

Wheelbarrow race

Group the children into pairs behind a starting line.

While one child lies face down on the ground, the other stands behind and, on starter's orders, takes hold of his partner's ankles (the child on the ground supports himself on his hands with arms outstretched) and the pair must 'wheelbarrow' to the finish line.

The winning pair receives a prize, the remaining children receive a small token.

Build a wall

YOU WILL NEED:
Coloured wooden blocks, sufficient for each child

Predetermine the dimensions of the wall according to the number of children and relay these instructions to the children, for example three rows of three bricks, so that both teams build the same shape.

Divide the children into two teams and have them stand in a row. Position a pile of 'bricks' at one end of the row, and provide a level surface at the other end of the row.

On starter's orders, the child at the front of each row lifts a brick and passes it down the line to the last child, who places the brick in position to construct a wall.

The child who has just positioned the brick runs to the front of the row and the process continues until each child has had a turn to place a brick and the wall is built. The first team to finish wins a prize, while the rest receive a small token.

Sand pit

YOU WILL NEED:
Sand pit or child's wading pool,
  filled with clean sand
Construction toys

Use yellow and black construction tape to demarcate an area where children may play in the sand with toys that are provided while they wait for all the children to arrive, and also between other activities.

Quick-setting cement

YOU WILL NEED:
Pile of clean sand
2 x large containers
2 x broad planks supported by bricks
2 x Hula Hoops
2 x plastic buckets

Position a pile of sand at one end of the play area, with the large containers at the other end. Lay out two obstacles between these two areas:
– Support a broad plank on two bricks, one at each end, which the children must walk across.
– Lay a Hula Hoop on the ground (an open manhole), which the children must jump over.
Divide the children into two teams and provide each team with a plastic bucket.

On starter's orders, the first child in each team must run to the pile of sand, fill the bucket and run to empty the sand into the large container.

The child then returns with the empty bucket and hands it to the next child who repeats the process. The race continues until each child has had a turn.

The team to finish first, with the most sand in the container, is the winner.

PARTY FOOD

Happy homes

Party Cupcakes (page 153)
Icing (page 152) – colour of choice
Liquorice Allsorts™
Desiccated coconut, coloured green
Coloured balls

1. Bake the cupcakes according to the recipe and allow to cool.
2. Coat with a layer of icing and then use a contrasting colour to ice a house.
3. Use Liquorice Allsorts™ to decorate as illustrated.
4. Sprinkle with coconut for the grass and add the flower using coloured balls.

Foreman Freddie

Sugar paste, coloured orange
Round orange sweets
Wafer ice-cream cones
Small sweets of choice
Marie biscuits or Rich Tea™ biscuits
Icing (page 152) – yellow, orange, red
Pretzel bows
Silver balls

1. Use the sugar paste to mould a construction helmet onto the round orange sweet.
2. Fill the cone with small sweets, then seal the broad end with a Marie or tea biscuit that has been coated with icing. Upend the cone so that it stands on the biscuit base, and cut the tip off the cone. Coat the cut end with icing and attach the head.
3. Carefully cut the arms from a pretzel and attach to the cone using a small dab of icing.
4. Using a star nozzle, pipe a ring of stars around the edge of the cone and Marie or tea biscuit to secure.
5. Pipe on a tie and a pair of trousers as illustrated.
6. Place blobs of icing in position for the eyes and attach the silver balls. Pipe the mouth as illustrated.

Dumping debris

Icing (page 152) – yellow, white
Wafer biscuits
Candy sticks
Jelly Babies™
Flat round sweets
Small gum drops

1. Apply a layer of icing to one wafer biscuit (this will form the base of the truck).
2. Cut a second wafer biscuit in half. Sandwich the two halves together with a thin layer of icing and place on top of and across the first wafer biscuit to form the cab of the truck.
3. Cut the candy sticks to size and place around the edge of the first biscuit, behind the cab section, to create the loading area of the truck.
4. Ice the top of the cab to match the base and ice the sides and front in white to make the windows.
5. Cut two Jelly Babies™ in half at the waist. Cut the back off the remaining section and discard. Stick the front of the sweet in place in the front windows to create a driver and passenger.
6. Add the round sweets for the wheels, and the gum drops for the headlights and a top emergency light.
7. Add a 'cargo' of choice (e.g. round vermicelli, hundreds and thousands, Mini Smarties™) to the loading area.

Other food ideas

Cocktail sausages with Mustard Dip (page 154).
Builder's brew: carbonated cold drinks in yellow or orange plastic mugs.
Sandwiches with selected fillings, cut into squares and triangles and reassembled to form house shapes.
Week's wages: foil-covered chocolate coins.

BUILDER'S DREAM CAKE

2 x Basic Cake (page 152) – two 330 mm x 260 mm cakes
Icing (page 152) – white, yellow
Mini chocolate slabs for bricks (or cut up a large thin slab into equal-sized rectangles)
Pretzel sticks for the door and the windowsills
Banana-shaped sweet for the door handle
Liquorice stick for the roof beams
Small clear plastic container for the cab of the crane
Small plastic toy doll for the crane driver
Candy stick with a cord attached
Flake® chocolate strips for the roof
Desiccated coconut, coloured green
About two Marie biscuits or Rich Tea™ biscuits, crushed
Silver vermicelli for the pile of building material
Sugar paste, coloured grey
Plastic trees
Toy construction vehicles

1. Bake the cakes according to the recipe and allow to cool.
2. Divide each cake in half by cutting widthways across the centre.
3. Place the four layers one on top of the other and secure with icing between each layer. Round off the edges to give a neater appearance.
4. Ice a section of the front and the adjoining side with white icing and place chocolate 'bricks' in position as illustrated.
5. Cover the rest of the cake with yellow icing.
6. Use pretzel sticks, trimmed down slightly, to create the door and position a sweet for the handle.
7. Use pretzel sticks for the windowsills and pipe the panes with white icing.
8. Cut five small portions off a liquorice stick and use for the roof beams.
9. Insert an upturned plastic container, together with the toy doll, on the top layer for the crane. The candy stick has the 'bricks' attached by means of a cord.
10. Place the Flake® strips on the roof, leaving a bundle lying about to create an unfinished appearance.
11. Scatter the green coconut to resemble the grass, and use the crushed Marie or tea biscuits for the sandy section. Position a pile of silver vermicelli to resemble builder's sand.
12. Position a thin strip of grey sugar paste for the road.
13. Position the toys and trees as indicated, using extra toy dolls if desired to create a busy building site.

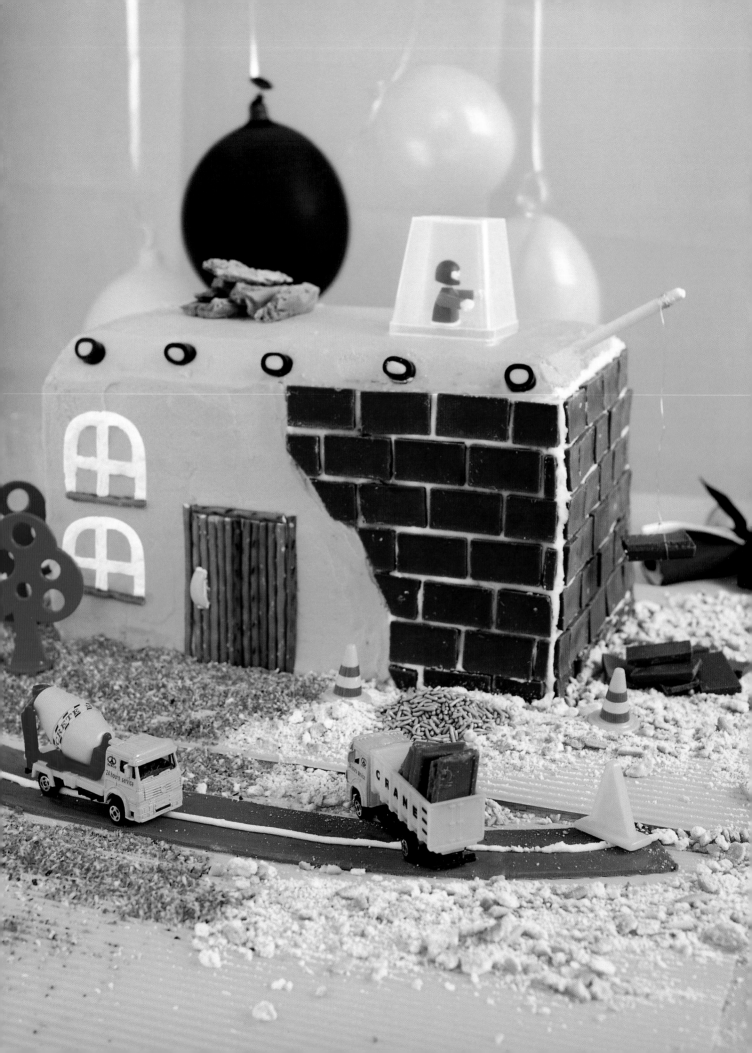

Face your

SETTING THE SCENE

* This party theme is aimed at older children. Parents may be concerned about the structure of this party, so allay their fears telephonically once the invitations have been distributed. You may want to check on food allergies at the same time with reference to some of the unusual food types that are used in the games.

* Cover the table with black crepe paper and place a ruche of soft red fabric down the centre.

* Drape red and black streamers from the centre of the ceiling to the corners of the room.

* Tie red and black balloons in bundles using curling ribbons and suspend in the corners of the room.

* Attach posters of extreme sporting activities to the walls, e.g. bungee jumping, sky diving, abseiling down buildings, rock climbing, and so on, and include shots of snakes and spiders, and other creepy crawlies.

* Serve the 'dry' party treats in sealed boxes, painted black with non-toxic craft spray, or covered with black paper, with a hole just big enough for the children to dare to put their hands through to grab a treat.

* Attach plastic snakes or spiders to the top of the boxes.

* Place toy snakes, scorpions and spiders in the bathroom and other rooms that will be used for the party.

Recommended age group: 9–12

Fears

INVITATIONS

YOU WILL NEED (PER INVITATION):
Empty baking powder tin or similar, sprayed black
with non-toxic craft spray
Aquarium gravel
Plastic toy snake
Notepaper
Elastic band
Red card

1. Place a little gravel in the tin together with the snake and the notepaper containing the party details (*see* Suggested wording).
2. Secure an elastic band around the neck of the tin and attach a card bearing the guest's name, and stating: 'Overcome your fear: dare to open the jar for details.'

SUGGESTED WORDING
Dare to show no fear at (birthday child's name)'s party!
Challenge site: (address)
Missions start: (starting time of party)
Missions end: (party ends)
RSVP: stunt co-ordinator at (phone number) by (date)
Dress: old clothes and sport shoes

TREAT BAGS

YOU WILL NEED:
Craft glue
Plastic toy snakes
Wooden clothes pegs
Brown paper bags
Felt-tip marker

1. Glue the snake to the clothes peg.
2. Fold down the top of the bag and clip the clothes peg over it to secure.
3. Write the child's name across the front of the bag.

GAMES AND ACTIVITIES

Lay out an obstacle course. Children must go from one station to the next as follows:

Station 1 –
Curb a ravenous appetite?

Provide three bowls of food with plenty of clean plastic spoons. Display the menu (without the substitute list, of course) and have the children draw numbers from a hat to determine which of the three bowls they have the privilege of sampling!

BOWL 1: CONGEALED BLOOD WITH TICKS AND MAGGOTS
congealed blood = cooked oats porridge coloured red with food colouring or tomato sauce
ticks = raisins
maggots = Rice Krispies®

BOWL 2: SNAKE VENOM WITH SCORPION TAILS AND FISH EYES
snake venom = puréed broccoli
scorpion tails = chopped gherkins
fish eyes = peeled grapes or litchis

BOWL 3: TARANTULAS WITH BLOOD CLOTS AND WORMS
tarantulas = pickled calamari tentacles
blood clots = red glacé cherries
worms = thinly sliced canned peaches

After choosing which bowl to sample, the children must draw numbers from a hat to decide their place in the queue. On their turn, each child is blindfolded and must take a spoonful from their respective bowl.

As they finish, the children are allowed to cheer on those still awaiting their turn. All the children who complete the challenge receive a small token.

Station 2 –
Crossing the snake pit!

Support a long plank on a layer of bricks. Make sure this is very stable. Positions are again determined by numbers drawn from a hat and the children are told that they have to walk across a pit of spitting snakes and sharp-toothed rats.

One by one, each child is blindfolded before entering the playing area, where they must walk along the plank, while the rest of the children await their turn in a separate area. As they walk along the plank, they are sprayed using water pistols (spitting snakes) and their legs are brushed by furry fabric (the rats).

Once they have completed the obstacle, they remain in the playing area to cheer and encourage the remaining children, as they complete their task.

Those who complete the challenge receive a small prize, the rest receive a token.

Station 3 –
Don't squash the slugs!

Spread two large blankets on the ground and lay a sheet of bubble wrap, preferably the larger bubble type, under each.

Divide the children into two teams. The children have to crawl under the blanket to the other side without popping the wrap. Noisy crawlers are eliminated.

The winning team is the one with the highest number of successful crawlers – the team members each receive a small prize, while the remaining children receive a token.

Station 4 – Can-can walk

Make the 'walking cans' as follows:

Use four large, clean, empty and sturdy food cans and make two small holes in each, opposite each other just below the unopened end.

Cut four pieces of strong string, each of sufficient length to be threaded through the two holes and to reach up to the children's hands. Knot the ends together.

The children place one foot on each tin and use the string to lift the tins as they walk.

Divide the children into two teams, lined up one behind the other, and provide each team with a pair of 'walking cans'. Instruct the children to:

– Negotiate a snake pit – a shallow dugout containing plastic snakes, then
– Climb over a length of rope suspended about 300–400 mm off the ground, then
– Crawl through a spider colony – use a large cardboard box with top and bottom removed to make a tunnel, and hang artificial spider webs containing plastic spiders inside the tunnel, then
– Race back to the team and hand the cans to the next child, who starts the process all over again. The first team to finish wins a prize.

Station 5 – Counting worms

Provide each child with two small bowls, one containing cooked spaghetti strands (add food colouring to the water in which the spaghetti is cooked) and the other empty. (For added effect, use two different colours, e.g. red for the spaghetti bowl and yellow for the empty bowl.) Add a few plastic flies to the spaghetti. If the party is in the evening, use glow-in-the-dark insects.

Instruct the children to sit in a circle with their hands clasped behind their backs. On starter's orders, they must transfer one strand of spaghetti at a time to the clean bowl using only their mouths. When the time is up, the child who has the most spaghetti in the clean bowl wins a prize. If there is a tie, the game continues until there is a winner.

PARTY FOOD

Spider's choice

Plastic toy spiders
Ice cube tray
Water
Carbonated juice of choice

1. Place the toy spiders in an ice cube tray, add water and freeze.
2. Add an ice block to each drink just before serving.
3. The children get to keep their spiders.

Slithering jelly

Sour worms or snake-shaped sweets
Small transparent serving cups
Jelly (quantity depends on number of children)
Plastic fly attached to a plastic spoon with craft glue

1. Place the sweet/s (quantity depends on the size of the sweet) in the base of the serving cup.
2. Mix the jelly according to the package instructions and pour into the serving cup.
3. Set in the fridge and serve with the plastic spoons.

Reaching the summit!

Wafer ice-cream cones
Sweets of choice
Marie biscuits or Rich Tea™ biscuits
Icing (page 152) – colour of choice
Liquorice strips
Thread (optional)
Small dolls
Toothpicks
Sprinkling of desiccated coconut
Large dome-shaped sugared jelly sweets

1. Fill the cone with sweets and cover with a Marie or tea biscuit that has been coated with icing. Upend so that the biscuit forms the base.
2. Make a hole in the top of the cone and insert one end of the liquorice strip, adding a small blob of icing to secure. Allow the liquorice to hang down the cone.
3. Coat the cone with icing, lifting the liquorice as necessary.
4. If necessary, attach one end of a piece of thread around the doll's wrist and the other around the end of a toothpick. Attach the toothpick to the top of the cone.
5. Wedge the doll's feet firmly into the cone. Allow the liquorice to dangle as if it is being held.
6. Sprinkle the summit with coconut (snow).
7. Cut the jelly sweet in half and skewer it onto the top of the toothpick to resemble a flag.

A rat's star choice!

Cheese slices
Small star-shaped cookie cutter
Small plastic toy rats
Shredded lettuce

1. Cut out stars from the cheese using the cookie cutter.
2. Place a toy rat on top of each piece of cheese and serve on a bed of finely shredded lettuce.

Striking ice cream

Ice cream
Jellied snake-shaped sweets
Toothpicks
Small sweets of choice

1. Coil the snake and skewer it with a toothpick to hold its shape. Set aside until ready to serve.
2. Place a scoop of ice cream in a bowl, cup or cone, sprinkle with sweets and insert the snake.

Snacksational spiders

Large polystyrene ball
Black non-toxic craft spray paint
Black pipe cleaners
2 x googly eyes
Sliced cocktail sausages
Cheese cubes
Coloured cocktail onions
Sliced gherkins
Pineapple chunks
Toothpicks

1. To make the spider, cut the polystyrene ball in half and spray it black. Allow to dry.
2. Place the ball cut side down, and add pipe cleaners for the legs. Attach the googly eyes.
3. Skewer the food onto the toothpicks and stick into the spider. Serve with dips of choice.

A T... T... T... Tarantula!

Party Cupcakes (page 153)
Icing (page 152) – blood red
Tarantula-shaped sweets
Desiccated coconut, coloured black

1. Bake the cupcakes according to the recipe and allow to cool completely.
2. Coat with a layer of red icing and attach the tarantula sweet. Sprinkle with coconut.

SNAKES ALIVE! CAKE

2 x Basic cake (page 152) – two 330 mm x 260 mm cakes
Icing (page 152) – colour of choice
Wafer biscuits
Doll – male or female
Snake sweets
2 x banana-shaped sweets for the handcuffs
Candy sticks
Gold or silver balls
Sprinkling of vermicelli

1. Bake the cakes as per the recipe and allow to cool completely.
2. Cut a snake trough from one of the cakes (the size will depend on the size of the doll), about 200 x 80 mm. Reserve the cut-out section.
3. Coat the other cake with a layer of icing and place the cake with the cut-out on top of this. Ice the whole cake.
4. Line the inside of the trough with wafer biscuits, cut to size.
5. Remove the doll's legs and insert the torso into the trough.
6. Cut the reserved piece of cake in half horizontally and place back in the trough, cut to fit, and wedged against the doll for support.
7. Add the snakes to the trough, curling them around the doll for effect.
8. Position the banana-shaped sweets on the doll's wrists for the handcuffs and secure with little blobs of icing.
9. Place pegs (candy sticks) in the cake near the hands and attach the handcuff chains (gold or silver balls) to this.
10. Place the supports (candy sticks) around the edge of the cake and attach the chains (gold or silver balls) to complete the effect.
11. Sprinkle the top of the cake with vermicelli.

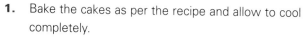

RECIPES

BASIC CAKE

Makes 1 x rectangular cake measuring 330 x 260 mm; OR 1 x round cake measuring 250 mm diameter; OR 2 x round cakes measuring 200 mm diameter.

4 eggs
300 g (300 ml) white sugar
2½ cups (625 ml) cake (plain) flour
4 tsp (20 ml) baking powder
a pinch of salt
¾ cup (180 ml) oil
¾ cup (180 ml) water
1 tsp (5 ml) vanilla essence

1. Preheat the oven to 180 °C (350 °F, gas mark 4).
2. Beat the eggs, then gradually add the sugar and beat until thick and pale.
3. In a separate bowl, sift the flour, baking powder and salt together.
4. In another bowl, lightly whisk the oil, water and vanilla essence to combine.
5. Gently fold the dry ingredients, alternately with the liquid, into the egg mixture.
6. Depending on your requirements, pour the cake mixture into the required greased cake tin(s).
7. Bake for 25–30 minutes. To test whether the cake is baked through, insert a skewer into the centre of the cake. If it comes out clean, it is done.
8. Turn out onto a rack to cool before icing.

ICING

This is sufficient to ice the basic cake, but for larger cakes, and particularly where the star nozzle is used, the quantity will have to be doubled.

100 g white margarine, at room temperature
2 cups (500 ml) icing sugar, sifted
± 5 tsp (25 ml) boiling water
½ tsp (2.5 ml) vanilla essence

1. Mix together the margarine and sifted icing sugar.
2. Add the boiling water a little at a time, and mix until the desired consistency is obtained.
3. Add the vanilla essence.
4. Once the icing has been mixed, it may be coloured by adding powdered colouring, blending in small quantities (about ¼ tsp) at a time, until the desired shade is obtained. Liquid colouring may be used if preferred, but care should be taken that the consistency does not become too runny.

For chocolate icing:
Add 2 Tbsp (30 ml) sifted cocoa powder to the icing sugar and proceed as above.

EASY BISCUITS

MAKES ABOUT 24 (DEPENDS ON SHAPE)
125 g butter
½ cup (125 ml) castor sugar
1 tsp (5 ml) vanilla essence
1 egg, beaten
2 cups (500 ml) cake (plain) flour
4 Tbsp (60 ml) cornflour
1 tsp (5 ml) baking powder
a pinch of salt

1. Preheat the oven to 180 °C (350 °F, gas mark 4).
2. Beat together the butter and castor sugar until pale.
3. Add the vanilla essence and egg.
4. Add the sifted dry ingredients and knead well to form a stiff dough.
5. Roll out on a lightly floured board to a thickness of 3–4 mm.
6. Cut into shapes.
7. Bake on a greased baking tray for 10–12 minutes until lightly browned.
8. Leave to cool completely before icing.
9. The dough may be prepared in advance and frozen until required (will keep for 4–6 weeks).

NOTE: Extra-large eggs (61–68 g) have been used throughout.

PARTY CUPCAKES

MAKES ABOUT 20
1½ cups (375 ml) self-raising flour
1 tsp (5 ml) baking powder
a pinch of salt
¾ cup (180 ml) sugar
2 eggs
½ cup (125 ml) oil
½ cup (125 ml) milk
1 tsp (5 ml) vanilla essence

1. Preheat the oven to 180 °C (350 °F, gas mark 4).
2. Mix the dry ingredients together.
3. Beat the eggs lightly and add the oil, milk and vanilla essence.
4. Add to the dry ingredients and mix well.
5. Spoon the mixture into cookie cups (muffin cases) in a cookie tray, and bake for 12–15 minutes.
6. Leave to cool before icing.

MARSHMALLOW CONES

MAKES ABOUT 32
1 cup (250 ml) boiling water
2 Tbsp (30 ml) gelatine powder
3 cups (750 ml) castor sugar
2 egg whites
1 tsp (5 ml) vanilla essence
about 32 edible (wafer) cookie cups
hundreds and thousands

1. Add the boiling water to the gelatine and stir until dissolved.
2. Pour into a mixing bowl along with the castor sugar, egg whites and vanilla essence.
3. Beat well with an electric beater until white and slightly stiff.
4. Fill the cookie cups with the mixture and allow to set slightly before sprinkling with hundreds and thousands.

MERINGUES

MAKES ABOUT 36
4 egg whites
a pinch of salt
1½ cups (375 ml) castor sugar

1. Preheat the oven to 100 °C (200 °F, gas mark ¼).
2. Whisk the egg whites and salt until stiff and dry.
3. Gradually add half the sugar, and whisk until stiff peaks form.
4. Fold in the remaining sugar, gently but thoroughly.
5. Spoon about 2 tsp (10 ml) of the mixture onto baking trays lined with greaseproof paper, spaced about 80 mm apart.
6. Bake for 1 hour. Switch off the oven, keep the door shut, and leave the meringues to cool completely, preferably overnight.

Note: To colour meringues, fold in two to three drops of food colouring before spooning onto the baking tray.

CHOCOLATE CRISPIES

MAKES ABOUT 48 SMALL
120 g icing sugar
1½ Tbsp (22.5 ml) cocoa powder
2 cups (500 ml) Rice Krispies®
½ cup (125 ml) desiccated coconut
120 g butter

1. Mix together the icing sugar, cocoa powder, Rice Krispies® and coconut.
2. Melt the butter in a saucepan.
3. Pour the melted butter over the dry ingredients and stir well.
4. Spoon into paper cookie cups (muffin cases) and place in the fridge to set.

CHOCOLATE OAT DROPS

MAKES ABOUT 36
400 g sugar
25 g cocoa powder
½ cup (125 ml) milk
125 g butter
300 g oats
100 g desiccated coconut

1. Mix together the sugar, cocoa, milk and butter in a saucepan, and stir over a low heat until the butter has melted and the sugar has dissolved.
2. Bring to the boil, stirring continuously, and then simmer for 1 minute.
3. Remove from the heat and add the oats and coconut. Mix well.
4. Drop tablespoonfuls of the mixture onto a baking tray lined with greaseproof paper and place in the fridge to set.

MARSHMALLOW FLOWERS

Coat a pair of kitchen scissors and your fingertips with icing sugar to prevent sticking.

Slice each marshmallow into four or five rounds, depending on size, and pinch and pull each slice at both ends to resemble a petal. Arrange the petals in a circle and place a sweet in the centre.

MINI MEATBALLS

MAKES ABOUT 30

500 g extra lean beef mince

1 onion, finely chopped

1 clove garlic, crushed

1 thick slice of stale white or
brown bread, crusts removed,
crumbed

1 Tbsp (15 ml) chutney

1 Tbsp (15 ml) brown vinegar

salt and pepper to taste

a pinch of mixed dried herbs

cake (plain) flour for dusting

1 egg, beaten

cooking oil for frying

1. Mix together the mince, onion, garlic, breadcrumbs, chutney, vinegar, seasoning and herbs.
2. Roll the mixture into walnut-sized balls.
3. Coat the meatballs with flour, then brush with beaten egg.
4. Fry in oil over medium heat, turning frequently, for 6–8 minutes until done.

AVOCADO DIP

MAKES 1 CUP (250 ML)

1 ripe avocado, peeled, pip
removed, mashed

½ cup (125 ml) thick mayonnaise

salt and pepper to taste

dash of lemon juice

Mix together all the ingredients and refrigerate.

SAUSAGE PIES

MAKES 8–10

1 x 450 g packet ready-made
puff pastry, defrosted

500 g pork or beef sausages,
skinned

1 small onion, finely chopped

a pinch of mixed dried herbs

salt and pepper to taste

a little milk or water

1 egg, beaten

1. Preheat the oven to 180 °C (350 °F, gas mark 4).
2. Roll out the pastry on a lightly floured surface, then use a cookie cutter or a template of choice to cut out pairs of pastry.
3. Mix together the sausage meat, onion, herbs and seasoning.
4. Place a portion of the filling on a pastry cut-out, cover with a matching piece and brush the edges with a little milk or water. Seal the edges.
5. Brush with beaten egg and bake on a baking tray for about 20 minutes or until the pastry is browned.

Note: These pies may be baked in advance and reheated shortly before serving.

MUSTARD DIP

MAKES 1½ CUPS (375 ML)

4 eggs

4 Tbsp (60 ml) sugar

4 Tbsp (60 ml) vinegar

2 Tbsp (30 ml) mustard powder

½ tsp (2.5 ml) salt

about 4 Tbsp (60 ml) mayonnaise,
or more if a less tangy mixture
is preferred

1. Beat the eggs, then add the sugar, vinegar, mustard powder and salt.
2. Cook in a double boiler, whisking all the time until thickened.
3. Remove from the heat, cool, then add sufficient mayonnaise until the desired consistency is obtained.
4. Store in the fridge.

FRILLY DRINKING STRAWS

Cut aluminium foil or foil gift wrap into strips measuring 20 x 70 mm. Leave about 20 mm intact at one end, then cut the remaining 50 mm into very narrow strips. Wind the intact base around a straw, close to the tip, and secure with a piece of tape. Gently stroke the strips so that they hang backwards.

TEMPLATES

page 138

page 116

page 72

page 80

page 116

pages 115 and 117

page 16

page 32

page 34

page 18

page 94

page 26

page 132

page 64

page 95

page 48

page 49

page 134

156 TEMPLATES

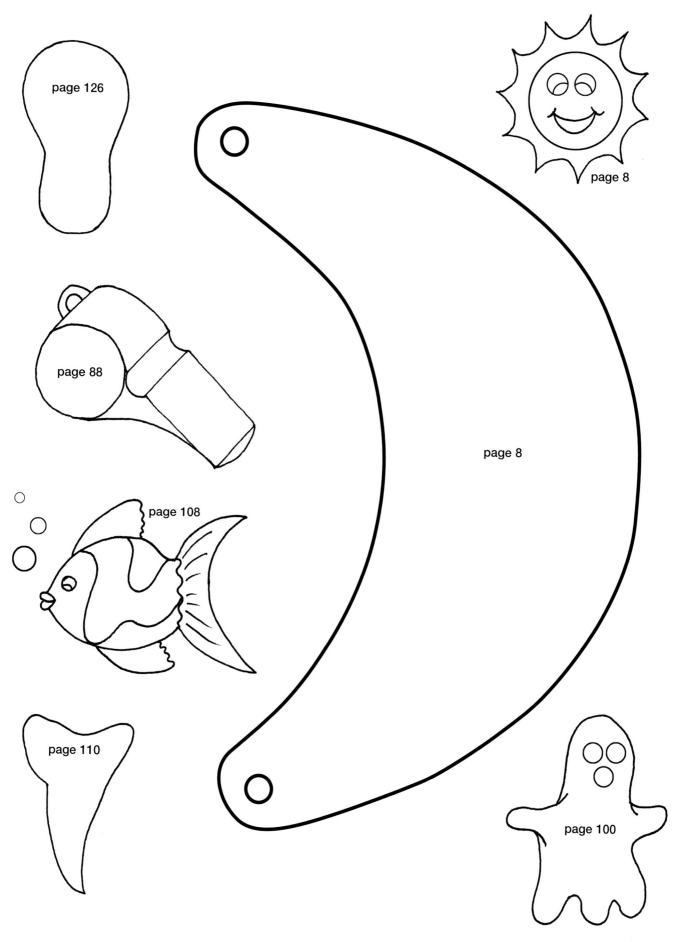

page 126

page 8

page 88

page 108

page 110

page 8

page 100

STOCKISTS

SOUTH AFRICA

BAKING SUPPLIES

The Baking Tin
– 52 Belvedere Rd, Claremont, Cape Town. Tel: (021) 671 6434.
– Shop 108, Glenwood Village, Cnr Hunt & Moore Rd, Glenwood, Durban. Tel: (031) 202 2224.
– Rochel Rd, Porridgevale, Port Elizabeth. Tel: (041) 363 0271.

Confectionery Extravaganza
Shop 48, Flora Centre, Ontdekkers Rd, Florida, West Rand, Johannesburg. Tel: (011) 672 4766.

South Bakels
19 Henry van Rooijen St, Bloemfontein. Tel: (051) 432 8446.

TOYS/ACCESSORIES

Factory Toy Shop
250 Voortrekker Rd, Parow. Tel: (021) 939 8938.

Plastics for Africa (toys, small plastic containers)
3b Montague Dr, Montague Gardens. Tel: (021) 551 5790.

The Plastics Warehouse (plastic sphere sets, toys)
26 Northumberland Rd, Bellville. Tel: (021) 948 3042.

The Crazy Store
– Sanlam Centre, Pretoria Rd, Randburg, Johannesburg. Tel: (011) 787 0048.
– 308 Sanlam Centre, Durban. Tel: (031) 709 6707.

PACKAGING

Merrypak & Print Packaging Warehouse (gift bags, ribbons, party boxes)
– 45 Morningside Rd, Ndabeni, Cape Town. Tel: (021) 531 2244.
– 21 Bridlington Rd, Seaview, Durban. Tel: (021) 465 2719.

Bellville Packaging (disposable cake domes, disposable plates, brown paper packets)
99 Voortrekker Rd, Bellville. Tel: (021) 949 7768.

FABRICS, RIBBONS, ETC.

Crafters One Stop Shop (craft supplies, googly eyes, sequins, small shells)
Checkers Hyper N1 City, Goodwood. Tel: (021) 595 2635.

Fabric City Wholesalers (fabrics, ribbons)
32 Sir Lowry Rd, Cape Town. Tel: (021) 462 1287.

Home Craft Fabric Paint and Accessories
35 Morningside Rd, Ndabeni, Cape Town. Tel: (021) 531 9425.

Arts, Crafts and Hobbies
72 Hibernia St, George. Tel: (044) 874 1337.

Maridadi Crafts
Shop 4 Centurion Mall, Centurion, Pretoria. Tel: (012) 663 4030.

Resia Hobbies and Crafts
Jo Gordge, 713 Kinsway, Athlone Park, Amanzimtoti. Tel: (031) 904 3622.

SWEETS/CHOCOLATES

Giant Sweet Wholesalers
3 Benbell Ave, Epping 1, Cape Town. Tel: (021) 534 5925.

Sweets from Heaven
Branches countrywide.

UNITED KINGDOM

Consult the Yellow Pages for cake decorating and party supplier shops.

Culpitt Ltd (baking supplies)
Jubilee Industrial Estate, Ashington, Northumberland NE63 8UQ. Tel: 01670 814545
www.culpitt.com

London Sugarart Centre (baking supplies)
12 Selkirk Rd, London SW17 0ES. Tel: 020 8767 8558
Fax: 020 8767 9939

Toys R Us (toys, games)
Freepost Nat 3362, Gateshead NE10 8BR.
www.toysrus.co.uk
Stores nationwide.

Woolworths (toys, sweets, chocolates)
Tel: 0845 608 1100
www.woolworths.co.uk
Stores nationwide.

Paperchase (gift bags, ribbons, party boxes)
213–215 Tottenham Court Rd, London W1T 7PS.
www.paperchase.co.uk
Stores nationwide.

Hobbycraft (craft supplies)
7 Enterprise Way, Aviation Park, Bournemouth International Airport, Christchurch, Dorset BH23 6HG.
Tel: 01202 596100
www.hobbycraft.co.uk
Stores nationwide.

John Lewis (fabrics, ribbons from haberdashery department)
Oxford St, London W1A 1EX.
www.johnlewis.com
Contact head office for store locations.

INDEX

Page numbers in **bold** indicate photographs